THE POWER OF RELAXATION

THE POWER OF RELAXATION

Tanushree Podder

Viva Books

New Delhi | Mumbai | Chennai | Kolkata | Bangalore | Hyderabad | Kochi

First Published 2006
Reprint 2008

VIVA BOOKS PRIVATE LIMITED

4737/23 Ansari Road, Daryaganj, New Delhi 110 002
E-mail: vivadelhi@vivagroupindia.net, Tel. 42242200

Plot No. 76, Service Industries, Shirvane, Sector 1, Nerul, Navi Mumbai 400 706
E-mail: vivamumbai@vivagroupindia.net, Tel. 27721273, 27721274

Jamals Fazal Chambers, 26 Greams Road, Chennai 600 006
E-mail: vivachennai@vivagroupindia.net, Tel. 28290304, 28294241

B-103, Jindal Towers, 21/1A/3 Darga Road, Kolkata 700 017
E-mail: vivakolkata@vivagroupindia.net, Tel. 22836381, 22816713

7, Sovereign Park Apartments, 56-58, K. R. Road, Basavanagudi, Bangalore 560 004
E-mail: vivabangalore@vivagroupindia.net, Tel. 26607409, 26607410

101-102 Mughal Marc Apartments, 3-4-637 to 641, Narayanguda, Hyderabad 500 029
E-mail: vivahyderabad@vivagroupindia.net, Tel. 27564481, 27564482

Beevi Towers, First Floor, SRM Road, Kaloor, Kochi 682 018, Kerala
E-mail: vivakochi@vivagroupindia.net, Tel: 0484-2403055, 2403056

www.vivagroupindia.com

ISBN-10: 81-309-0271-0
ISBN-13: 978-81-309-0271-5

Published by Vinod Vasishtha for Viva Books Private Limited,
4737/23, Ansari Road, New Delhi-110 002.

Printed and bound by Raj Press, R-3, Inderpuri, New Delhi - 110012

Dedication

To Ajoy, who relaxes me completely in every sense of the word

Contents

Acknowledgements IX
Prologue XI

The Power of Relaxation **01**
Why Can't People Relax?
The Vulnerable Ones
Coping Strategies
Relaxation and the Brain Waves
The Art of Relaxation
The 'WHAT' Syndrome
Rejuvenation
The Need to Relax
Holistic Relaxation

Physical Relaxation **43**
The Importance of Physical Relaxation
Basic Relaxation Technique
Stretch the Stress Away
Progressive Muscle Relaxation
Slumber Power
Relaxing Sleep
Using the Five Senses
The Sense of Sight
Visualisation for Relaxation
The Sense of Hearing
Mantra Chanting
The Sense of Smell
Aromatherapy for Relaxation

The Sense of Taste
Calming Food
The Sense of Touch
Massage for Relaxation
The Relaxing Breath
Vigour and Vitality
Affirmations for Relaxation
Laughter and Relaxation
Shavasana

Mental Relaxation 129
Relaxation and Emotions
Detoxification of Emotions
The Power of Positive Thinking
A Calm State of Mind
Autogenic Training and Self-Hypnosis

Spiritual Relaxation 155
Detoxifying the Soul
Meditation
Relaxation and Spirituality
Toxic Thoughts
Prayer Power
Relaxation and the Art of Forgiveness

Recharging the Body, Mind and Soul 189
Powerful Relaxation Techniques
Rejuvenation and Energising Exercises

Assessment Exercises 209
Are You Stressed?
Assess Your Stress Level
How forgiving Are you?
What about Leisure?
Are You a Type A Personality?
The Final Word

ACKNOWLEDGEMENTS

The birth of each book involves the dedication of many people. From the person who acts as the sounding board to the editor who shares the pangs of birth as intensely as the author, each one is equally indispensable.

As usual, my husband has been the sounding board with whom I had many disagreements as we discussed the contents that needed to fit into the hundred odd pages of the manuscript. His patience is commendable.

I wouldn't have been able to complete the book without the presence of our man-Friday, Ravindra Arankar, who handled all the routine chores while I spent hours before the computer. A special round of thanks go to him for being my hands and feet, eyes and ears around the house.

This book couldn't have adorned the bookshelves without the great work put in by my editor.

Prologue

We are a part of the vast sea of humanity that is searching for the ultimate utopia, misled by the thought that successful careers and wads of currency will buy us a place there. So, in a bid to accumulate those wads and reach the pinnacle of our successful careers, we have surrendered our peace of mind, unblemished souls and physical health.

The 24x7x365 culture has invaded this planet. Companies proudly flaunt the non-stop work culture, slave driving their employees with promises of more greenbacks to compensate for the mental peace and happiness they have lost.

The taut muscles, the rigid jaws and the overstrained nerves are a few pointers to our unrelenting torture of the self. We rush to the healing centres, spiritual gurus, healers, and spend thousands of rupees to learn the art of de-stressing and breathing, which should come naturally to us. We practise the things we learn for a couple of weeks, and then it is back to square one. We bicker, backstab, envy, hurt and tread on others' toes, do anything to get ahead. We join the never-ceasing race once again. It is the survival of the fittest, after all. Anyone who doesn't join the race gets left behind, and so we run. We forget that the winner in a rat race still remains a rat. We run and keep running till we are totally exhausted. The vicious circle goes on without stopping till one day our bodies can't run any longer, we are seized with weak bodies, demented minds and saddened souls. And one fine day, it is time for us to bid goodbye to this planet. Our time is up, and we have to keep the ultimate appointment with our maker!

We leave behind so many unfinished tasks, so many dreams and so many desires. The treasure and the wealth, which we pursued with such a single-minded approach, remain behind, totally useless. It is the wealth that we amassed with great labour and sacrifice. For these pieces of worthless papers we gave up so many glorious years of our lives. We subjected ourselves to untold miseries, frustrations, reckless drive and ill health. And finally, when we meet the maker and he asks us, 'Did you enjoy the precious life I granted you? Did you derive pleasure from the infinitely beautiful nature I gifted you?' we will just gape and bow our heads shamefacedly. Is this why the gift of life came our way?

Sounds depressing, doesn't it? It need not be this way. Life can still be beautiful. It can be a joyful experience and a soul-lifting journey replete with pleasure and happiness. It can leave us satisfied and content. Then we can answer our maker truthfully, 'It was a beautiful experience. Thank you God for giving me this precious gift of life.'

Ask anyone, and they'll tell you that they are stressed beyond belief, most of the time. Where is the time to relax? They will scoff if you talk about slowing out of the race. Fifty years back, people retired from work and led a peaceful life, but today there is no retirement. Retired people begin their career afresh, joining the rat race once more and competing with the younger generation. From the child who is burning the midnight oil for a glorious future to the woman who is desperately working to balance her home and career, and the man who is slogging away at his career at the cost of his family, everyone is a part of the relentless chase. There is no time to pause and take stock. The fear that the slightest hesitation or breather could get them trampled under the million feet that are racing ahead stops them from even contemplating it.

Yet, the same people are forced to pause when their tired bodies and exhausted minds throw up the white flag of surrender. Hypertension, diabetes or coronary ailment will eventually force them to halt – as will neurosis and depressive states of mind. By then, it would be too late. The doctors will sound the death knell with their dire diagnoses. What follows is a string of regrets of what could have been. How life could have been beautiful and how they could have enjoyed life had it not been for the thoughts of the future.

Why wait for that day? Why not begin enjoying the gift of life right now? Would it not be foolish to ruin today in contemplation of a glorious tomorrow? For who knows what tomorrow may hold for us, anyway?

Pause, think and introspect. Where are you heading? What do you seek? And what is the ultimate price that needs to be paid for the elusive utopia?

You may form your own answers to these questions, but most people will say that they are seeking happiness. If it is happiness you are seeking, how will you find it? What is the first step that you need to take in order to move out of the rut? I would say, begin with a programme for relaxing your body, mind and soul.

For some people relaxation comes naturally, but for others it has to be brought in with effort. Some of us are beautifully adapted to the pace of their lives while many of us struggle to cope with the demands life makes on us. Is it genetic, this natural calm?

I would like to believe so. Some of us who have managed to retain their tranquillity can trace it back to their parents who remained in a calm and composed state through most of their ordeals. Those of us who are short-tempered and restless can also trace that trait back to one of our parents.

What is it that makes some people so capable of handling stress and balancing their lives so beautifully, even if they are running business empires?

Although these people are exposed to the same hazards, they have learnt the art of controlling their stress levels. Their reaction to the same life situation is very different from a person who is unable to keep his stress under control. It is not the situation but the reaction to it that determines the stress level.

It is to help you live your life to the hilt that this book has been written. Life is not about toil and ambition alone; it is about enjoying each moment. It is about learning to relax and take things in the stride. It is about the blissful enjoyment of the years granted to us on this planet.

Believe me, you will be more successful, happier and contented if you pursue your career, relationships and ambitions in a relaxed manner.

—Tanushree Podder

CHAPTER ONE

The Power of Relaxation

Relaxed people are smarter, healthier, more successful, sharp thinkers, beautiful, popular and have better career graphs. They make better lovers. Their memory is better and they function more efficiently. These people make a remarkable difference to the world and are the ultimate winners. All this does not mean that successful people are not stressed. It simply means that they are able to cope with the stress in an equally successful manner.

A relaxed mind is at its creative best. It comes up with solutions to most problems, copes wonderfully with the demands made on it and is superbly agile.

Does This Surprise You?

It shouldn't. Why are they smarter? They are smarter simply because a relaxed brain works at its optimum level. It is a well-known fact that stress impairs our brain functions and memory.

They are healthier because they are relaxed. Stressed bodies are deficient in oxygen, which in turn reduces vitality. A stressed system leads to partial elimination causing constipation, messes up digestive functions, which in turn causes acidity and other problems.

Relaxed people are more successful and popular because their tempers are under control. Tense people have short tempers that flare up easily, leading to broken relationships and unpopularity in social and work sphere. Their impatience and restlessness adversely affect their careers.

Relaxation is an antidote to stress. So, all these problems are eliminated the moment a person is relaxed. Having said that, let me stress that one has to achieve a naturally-relaxed state of mind and body to reap all the benefits.

Holistic relaxation brings mental clarity, smart thinking and improved memory along with a host of other benefits. The vitality and energy of a relaxed body is at its peak. All the systems work with renewed energy after complete repose. The digestive system is at its happiest, the elimination system is at its peak, the respiratory system performs superlatively and the heart remains healthy.

The very process of breathing is rejuvenated. When we undergo a stressful period, the amount of oxygen intake suffers, since our breath becomes shallow and uneven. Relaxation brings with it healthy breathing, where the oxygen-rich breath enters our system to recharge our cells to their fullest vitality.

The blood pressure stabilises as the blood flows smoothly through the body. The enrichment of blood to the brain makes it work better, resulting in sharp thinking and improved memory. The harnessing of the energies vitalises the mind. The kidneys work better, helping in the elimination process.

The skin, in turn, becomes flawless as the elimination and respiratory system, two major contributors to its health, begin to work at their optimum level.

You become beautiful! You remain forever young. What more could you want? But wait, there is more.

Along with your complexion, the happiness factor perks up significantly. The feel-good factor goes up by leaps and bounds as the mind and body are at their best. The muscles are more relaxed, leading to less aches and pains. The best part is that holistic relaxation has a strong anti-ageing effect on the body. Wrinkles and worry lines arrive much later in life when a person is relaxed. One has to simply observe a stressed person's life vis-à-vis a relaxed person's life to know the difference.

Relaxation strengthens the immune system, allowing the body to ward off diseases. It is able to heal itself faster and maintain a state of equilibrium.

The list does not end here. The sexual life takes an upward swing. Did you know that a relaxed body and mind is the first requisite of your sexual performance? Hormones surge in a relaxed body more efficiently than in a stressed out body. The problem of childlessness that is becoming a common phenomenon in working couples is more due to the stress factor than anything else.

Amazing, isn't it? There is more. The popularity graph goes up because a relaxed person is more tolerant and better company. He gets sought out in the social events, as people feel more comfortable in his company. This, in turn, affects the career and family life too.

Divorces, broken relationships, family problems are minimal in relaxed couples. The quality of relationships definitely improves since they make better parents, spouses and partners. A relaxed family is a happy family where children perform better, spouses understand each other and there is an aura of contentment in the house.

A relaxed mind tunes easily with God. It can connect better with spirituality. The soul is lighter, the mood congenial and the body willing to undertake the responsibilities the society and family thrust on us.

If all this sounds utopian, why wait to attain all this, just begin the process of relaxation. Get relaxed and rejuvenated!

Recap

- Relaxed people are smarter, healthier, more successful, sharp thinkers, beautiful, popular and have better career graphs. Their memory is better; they function more efficiently, make remarkable difference to the world and are the ultimate winners.
- Holistic relaxation makes all bodily systems work efficiently. Whether it is the circulatory, respiratory, elimination or reproduction system, all the processes operate at their peak level.
- Relaxed people are healthier because their immune system works at its peak, resisting all kinds of ailments.
- Sex life perks up.
- The anti-ageing effect of holistic relaxation is very real.
- The skin glows.
- The mind clears up with the better supply of oxygen due to improved respiration, and the brain sharpens. Memory improves significantly.
- The feel-good factor rises, as does the popularity level.
- The relationships get better, career zooms and you connect with God.
- The entire body goes through a period of rejuvenation.

Why Can't People Relax?

Sudhir Rane, a 45-year-old bank executive, suffered from his first heart attack, which proved to be strong enough to cause death. The diagnosis – he was working too hard, drinking too hard and worrying too hard.

Kalpana Sen, a 38-year-old creative director of an ad agency, discovered that she had developed lifestyle diabetes. The diagnosis – too many deadlines to keep – excessive smoking and insomnia.

Anurag Vaidyanathan, a 17-year-old school student, was taken for psychiatric treatment by his parents for suffering acute depression and suicidal tendencies. The diagnosis – the boy had been struggling too hard for admission into IIT.

Although these three people belong to different age groups, come from different backgrounds and have different lifestyles, the common thread that binds them is excessive stress. They are all striving to cope with the pressures heaped on them by various agencies.

People can't relax because they are too stressed and do not know how to de-stress. We all know that unhealthy levels of stress are bad for us. So much has been written about the 'S' word that nothing remains to be unravelled. Stress is bad, stress has to be controlled, stress factors have to be recognised and stressors eliminated. All that and more! It doesn't have to be spelt out that stress is something we all would like to handle better and control, but most of us find it unwieldy and uncomfortable.

When there are so many ill effects connected with stress, isn't it logical to wonder why we get stressed, in the first place?

Nature created the human body with an ability to tolerate a lot of stress. But we abuse our body and mind with much more rubbish than they can withstand. Most of us take more care of our cars than we take of our bodies.

The word 'stress' is taken from engineering jargon. In essence it means the deformation or change caused on a body by the internal forces that work on it. The maximum stress a body can withstand and still return to its normal state is known as its 'elastic limit'.

This applies to people too – an individual has his or her own elastic limit, both in terms of degree and type of stress. Just like the elastic can snap after it has reached the stretch limit, our bodies can snap too. It is when the body is put under long-term stress that it can reach its snapping point. If it does, the damage can be irreparable.

The lexicon defines stress as a body condition that occurs in response to actual or anticipated difficulties in life. Note the word – anticipated. Most of the time we live in the past or the future. We stress ourselves out imagining the future problems, anticipating difficulties that we are likely to suffer.

Stress isn't a bad thing when it is under control. In fact, it is quite desirable. Without it, we would not put in our best effort. Recent studies have revealed that stress can rejuvenate brain cells and delay dementia, but only when it is of the right kind and controlled in nature. It is only when it goes out of control that it begins to harm us. The art of stress management is to keep yourself at a level of stimulation that is healthy and enjoyable.

While there are dozens of reasons why a person may be stressed, there are several stressors that are common to most of us:

- **Survival Stress:** This may occur in cases where your survival or health is threatened, where you are put under pressure, or where you experience some unpleasant or challenging event. Adrenaline is released in your body and you' experience all the symptoms of your body preparing for 'fight or flight'.

- **Internally-Generated Stress:** This can come from anxious worrying about events beyond your control, from a tense, hurried approach to life, or from relationship problems caused by your own behaviour. It can also come from an 'addiction' to and enjoyment of stress.

- **Environmental and Job Stress:** Here your living or working environment causes the stress. It may come from noise, crowding, pollution, untidiness, dirt or other distractions. Alternatively, stress can come from events at work.

- **Fatigue and Overwork:** This kind of stress builds up over a long period. It can occur where you try to achieve too much in too little time, or where you are not using effective time management strategies.
- **Life Situations:** These would include events like death of a spouse or close relative. Such stress could also occur when we find ourselves in a totally new environment, surrounded by strangers.

Of all the stressors, the ones related to lifestyle and jobs are the most common. In fact, they form the bulk of stressors.

Aruna Varma, a software specialist, who is a close friend, came to me one morning. Over a cup of coffee, she confided about her high level of stress and the related health problems she was facing. 'I can't sleep. It is so tiresome. Nothing seems to help.' She was contemplating taking drugs that would help her sleep.

I vehemently opposed the idea. 'Let us not rush into such solutions. Instead, we could discuss the causes that are leading to insomnia. Perhaps, eliminating the cause could help,' I suggested.

Over a couple of hours, we discussed her relationships, environment, health and other facets of life. It was when we were talking about her career that the new job she had just taken came up for discussion. Slowly and carefully we began dissecting the elements that went with the job - we covered her colleagues, contents, job structure, duties, responsibilities, work environment, salary, almost everything we could think of. When we came to her boss, she got excited.

'It is my boss. I have got it. He is the one who is stressing me out.'

She went on to describe the lack of clarity in his expectations and spoke about the unclear objectives. We decided that she should discuss the problem honestly with her boss and seek solutions.

When I met her six months later, she still had some problems but she seemed more relaxed. It was the discussion and the measures that followed, which had made the difference.

A stress-free existence is perhaps a mirage. The pressures of modern living ensure that stress is always lurking in the background. It can't be eliminated, but one could try to control it.

The Vulnerable Ones

Some of us are more vulnerable to the stress disorders than others. Psychologists have divided people into two categories, the Type A and Type B personalities, based on their behaviour patterns. They have also devised a set of criteria by which people can be categorised under the two heads. Research has shown that there are certain kinds of individuals who suffer more from stress. They are unable to relax and remain on the verge of high stress levels almost all the time. They teeter between 6–10 in a scale of 1–10, rarely slipping below the mid-level. These people have been categorised as Type A individuals. On the other hand are the Type B, who are easy going, relaxed and more laid-back. This type is better adapted to the challenges of life situations and can handle stress more efficiently.

How does one differentiate between the two types?

Type A personalities are the strict, rigid and perfectionist types. Type B, on the other hand, is the relaxed kind of individual. Fundamentally, Type A kind grows out of having had to earn acceptance rather than being bestowed with it unconditionally. This person as a child was probably given conditional love, had a role model who was raised on conditional love, or both. There was a standard to be met, and if it was met there was acceptance and reward; if the standard wasn't met, then there was neither reward nor acceptance.

Although Type A individuals differ in all aspects from Type B, these folks have major problems around three key areas: time, money and emotions.

Type A and Time: Type A people have infinite problems with time. These personalities are obsessed with the value of time. They need to be everywhere on time; they need to avoid running out of time; they want to have a watch or clock handy, so they can measure time. They invest time; measure the value of time spent and time available to them. These individuals have problems with deadlines, as time limits can be very restrictive. Yet they feel they must work under deadlines and meet them too.

Type A and Money: Type A people have esteem issues, as they don't base their value on solid ground but rather on meeting standards. As such, they measure themselves and what they do by money. What's it worth, what did it cost, how much do they earn, have and spend? Money is their measure of achievement. They spend or give money as a way of showing love or affection. It is the major source of their empowerment and security. In relationships also, they use money as a medium of exchange and acceptance.

Type A and Emotions: Type A personalities may deny emotion or not know they have any. They may feel guilty for having or showing emotions, as this would deflect the importance of other elements like time and money. Since they are perfectionists, they strive to work for tangible things in life, and emotions, they feel, are a waste of time.

Little wonder, then, that a Type A individual suffers from higher stress levels than the others. Even a little variation in the schedule or change in lifestyle throws these people off gear. They find it difficult to adjust to change and like their lives to run on clockwork pattern. Paradoxically, this type is increasing in number in today's world. And that is the answer to why there is a growing stress level around us.

I recognise this type very well because I have grown up with one. My father definitely belongs to Type A. Unfortunately, I inherited the genes of Type A, to a large extent. It took me years of wilful effort to grow out of the stress-promoting habits and behaviour. I wouldn't claim to have beaten the stress levels completely, but I have definitely come a long way. I still work under deadlines set by myself; I also value time, maybe more than it deserves, but I have also learnt to meditate and breathe right. This has taken much of the stress off my mind. It has not been an easy victory, but one gets there, eventually, if one tries hard enough. Robin Sharma, author of the best-selling book *The Monk Who Sold His Ferrari* says: 'Never sacrifice happiness for achievement.' If only we would do so!

Recap

- The word 'stress' is taken from engineering jargon. In essence it means the deformation or change caused on a body by the internal forces that work on it.
- The lexicon defines stress as a body condition that occurs in response to actual or anticipated difficulties in life.
- Stress isn't a bad thing, when it is under control. In fact, it is quite desirable. Without it, we would not put in our best effort.
- Stress can be broadly categorised under four heads – survival stress, internally–generated stress, job stress, fatigue stress and life-situation stress.
- Job-related stress and relationship stress is the commonest kind of stress found in metropolitan cities.
- Two personality types were identified by the psychologists in order to define people's behaviours – Type A and Type B.
- Type A individuals are more stressed than Type B.

They have major problems with time, money, dirt and relationships.

Coping Strategies

The most common question people ask in magazines, doctor's clinics, social circles and over helplines is: 'How do I cope with my stress level?' While it would be nice to have a simple answer to that query, unfortunately, we all have different kinds of individual stressors that cannot be controlled through a common panacea which is applicable to everyone. Worst still is the fact that most people who discover their remedy do not stick with it. After the first burst of energetic application of the stress-busters, most of them revert to the old way of living, stress et al.

To put it simply, I would group the majority of stressors under three main heads. Altering these could make a sea change in your stress levels.

1. Your attitude
2. Your behaviour
3. Your lifestyle

1. Altering the Attitude: Largely, it is our attitude that is responsible for the way we react to any life situation. For instance, while Satish is more accepting, his wife, Anila, can't easily accept changes in her schedule or unseen circumstances in daily life. Even a minor matter like the sudden arrival of a guest can put her in a spin, and this can become a major stressor for her. This attitudinal difference is easily discernible in workplaces also. While one employee reacts calmly to the sudden changes in plans, the other can get totally baffled. How can one change one's attitude?

Attitude may be a hot word today, but it is all about the negative and the positive attitude. If you are positive, you have made it, and if you are negative, god help you!

Here is where the power of positive thinking and affirmation come into the picture. There is growing evidence about the efficacy of thought process on stress control.

2. Altering the Behaviour: People's behaviour very greatly. If you are the kind who gets agitated in a traffic jam, honking furiously and swearing at everyone, you need to examine your behaviour pattern. Let's face it, you will be stuck in the jam, there is no escaping. Look around you. You'll spot people tackling the situation in various ways. Some will be happily talking into their mobiles or nodding their heads to the beat of their favourite music, or even catching up with the news with their noses buried behind the papers. At the same time, you will see some who, like you, are seething with anger, tapping their feet with irritation, their teeth clenched, jaws set, as though they are on the war path.

You have a choice – tap your feet to the music or to the irritation seething within. It is this choice that you have to exercise. In life, there are hundreds of such situations, which demand resignation and not aggression. Accept the inevitable – it is less stressing.

Our behaviour in different situations reflects our mind-set. Behaviours are the responses one exhibits when confronted with situations that can be negative or positive. While some of us are exuberant and full of pep, responding to the happy moments with abandon, others may have a controlled response to the same events. Similarly, a tragic event or a negative situation may evoke strong response like depression in one person, while another may have a better grip on it. People who respond strongly get stressed when the situations are not in their favour, whilst the stoic ones can accept the unfavourable situations in a calm manner. Being able to alter the behavioural pattern can help in controlling stress to a large extent. There are certain techniques that are very effective in altering behaviour. For instance, expressing the feelings (ventilation) and developing a strong sense of humour are known to be wonderful anti-dotes to stress-forming behaviour.

3. Altering The Lifestyle: If you are a kind who love their hamburgers and pizzas downed with gallons of fuzzy aerated drink, spend more time at the desk than outdoors, and hate the very idea of working out, you need to examine your lifestyle. You are the number one on the hit list as far as bad health is concerned. Not only that, you are also the favourite prey for the stressors – both physical and emotional.

Lifestyle has become the biggest villain in the modern scenario. It is the number one cause of most diseases. Whether it is diabetes, heart problem or psychological problems like depression, the root of almost every other ailment can be traced back to unhealthy lifestyle. Lifestyle is a package that largely involves diet and exercise along with mind control. There are many effective ways of altering lifestyle that can lead to a healthier body as well as mind.

Practising calming influences like meditation, imagery and music, along with a rigorous change in diet, can largely help in controlling the ailments. Keep ample time for leisure. It has the biggest role to play in the control of stress.

Since all of us are not capable of controlling stress totally, we have to learn the 'art of relaxation'. Unfortunately, this is exactly the business that has spawned a millions-worth industry. Spiritual gurus, writers, therapists – you name it – are earning lakhs of rupees just teaching people the art of breathing and the art of relaxing. Strange as it may sound, people have forgotten to relax, just as they have forgotten to breathe right. Things which should occur naturally to human beings are getting difficult to perform, and this is where the smart ones are making money.

Happiness is intrinsically related to the relaxed state. A tense person finds it difficult to remain joyful. Happiness is a state when the three – mental, physical and emotional – elements are in balance. The same definition could hold true for relaxation too.

Relaxation and the Brain Waves

People are not fooling when they talk about brain waves. It is these waves that make all the difference in our moods, stress levels, creativity and reactions. The lower the waves, the calmer the mind.

There are four stages of consciousness during which our brain waves operate at different cycles. These stages are recorded by an electroencephalogram (EEG), which measures electrical impulses sent by neuron firings in the synapses of the brain. When the mind is very active, it works at 20–25 brainwave cycles per second. In an agitated state, the brainwaves can reach an alarming number of cycles while a calm and relaxed mind would produce brain waves as low as 4–8 cycles per second.

1. Beta Waves

In the Beta state, neurons fire abundantly, in rapid succession, helping you achieve peak performance. New ideas and solutions to problems flash like lightning into your mind. You are wide-awake and alert. Your mind is sharp, focused. It makes connections quickly, easily and you're primed to do work that requires your full attention.

Beta-centred programmes help you prepare to take an exam, play sports, give a presentation, analyse and organise information and other activities where mental alertness and high levels of concentration are key to your success. Beta waves range between 13–40 Hz. The Beta state is associated with peak concentration, heightened alertness, hand–eye coordination and visual acuity.

2. Alpha Waves

These are associated with relaxation, visualisation and creativity. When you are truly relaxed, your brain activity slows from the rapid patterns of Beta into the more gentle waves of Alpha. Your awareness expands. Fresh creative energy begins to flow. Fears vanish. You experience a liberating sense of peace and well-being. In biofeedback, Alpha training is most commonly recommended for the treatment of stress.

Alpha-centred programmes help you tap your creativity and are excellent for problem-solving, finding new ideas and practising creative visualisation. Choose Alpha programmes when you want to attain deep levels of relaxation that are essential to your health and well-being.

Alpha waves range between 7–12 Hz. This is a place of deep relaxation, but not quite meditation. In Alpha, we begin to access the wealth of creativity that lies just below our conscious awareness – it is the gateway, the entry point that leads into deeper states of consciousness.

3. Theta Waves

These waves stand for meditation, intuition and memory. Going deeper into relaxation, you enter the elusive and mysterious Theta state where brain activity slows almost to the point of sleep, but not quite. Theta is the brain state where magic happens in the crucible of your own neurological activity. Theta brings forward heightened receptivity, flashes of dreamlike imagery, inspiration and your long-forgotten memories. Theta can bring you deep states of meditation, a sensation of 'floating'. And, because it is an expansive state, in Theta, you may feel your mind expand beyond the boundaries of your body.

Theta rests directly on the threshold of your subconscious. In biofeedback, it is most commonly associated with the deepest levels of meditation. Theta also plays an important part in behaviour modification programmes and has been used in the treatment of drug and alcohol addiction. Finally, Theta is an ideal state for super-learning, re-programming your mind, dream recall and self-hypnosis.

Theta waves range between 4–7 Hz. Theta is one of the more elusive and extraordinary realms we can explore. It is also known as the twilight state, which we normally only experience fleetingly as we rise up out of the depths of Delta upon waking, or drifting off to sleep. In Theta, we are in a waking dream, vivid imagery flashes before the mind's eye, and we are receptive to information beyond our normal conscious awareness. Theta has also been identified as the gateway to learning and memory. Theta meditation increases creativity, enhances learning, reduces stress and awakens intuition and other extrasensory perception skills. Theta waves, even if achieved, are difficult to maintain.

4. Delta Waves

Delta waves represent detached awareness, healing and sleep. The Delta waves occur during the stage of deep sleep. They measure 4–6 cycles per second and there is more body movement and activity during this phase. After the first 'alpha rhythm' stage, the brain falls into a second stage of drowsiness, and a pattern of much slower, more irregular waves occurs. Then finally, the person falls into deep sleep, characterised on the EEG machine by big, deep 'delta waves', punctuated by small patches of shorter, faster waves, which are termed 'sleep spindles'. This state is known as 'orthodox sleep'.

Long, slow, undulating, Delta is the slowest of all four brain wave frequencies. Most commonly associated with deep sleep, certain frequencies in the Delta range also trigger the release of Human Growth Hormone so beneficial for healing and regeneration. This is why sleep – deep restorative sleep – the kinds that Delta frequencies help induce, is so essential to the healing process.

Delta is the brain wave signal of the subconscious, the seat from which intuition arises. That means Delta waves are not only an ideal choice for their sleep and deep regeneration potential, but also when you want to access your unconscious activity and help that wellspring of information flow to your conscious mind for clearing and for empowerment.

An easy way to understand the brain waves is to compare the four basic brain waves (Delta, Theta, Alpha, Beta) with the four gears on a car. Delta (the slowest wave) is first gear. Theta is second gear. Alpha is third gear. Beta is fourth gear. Just as we need all the four gears to drive a car, all the brain waves are required for optimum functioning of the brain. There is no one gear suited for every driving situation; similarly, no one brain wave is best for all of the challenges of life. We get into trouble if one of the gears on our car goes out, or if we forget to use some of the gears. Imagine driving a car, beginning with the first gear, and then shifting directly into fourth gear without bothering to use the second and third gears, not only will we get low fuel mileage but also high repair bills. The same is true of our brains. Sadly, many people often skip their second and third brain gears – the Theta and Alpha. The penalty for driving our brains in this manner is low productivity and high medical bills.

Let us see a common example that occurs in everyday life. We jump out of the bed from a deep sleep, during which the brain generates delta waves, with the pealing of the alarm. What follows is a feeling of stress and anxiety about being late, and we begin to rush about, trying to race time. All this happens with the Beta waves ruling the brain. Even as the groggy mind staggers out of its inertia, we quickly pour cups of coffee down the throat to force ourselves into wakefulness – more beta. The caffeine suppresses Theta and Alpha waves, all the while encouraging the Beta ones. There has been no gradual transition from the Delta to the Beta waves; it has been a swift switch from one to the other. All through the day we work under stress, pressure and deadlines – a surfeit of Beta. This continues until at night we fall exhausted into deep sleep, plunging into the Delta phase. There has hardly been any time for unwinding or relaxing, which would have given a bit more of the Alpha and Theta waves. Again, there has been no gradual transition. This actually happens to most people as they switch their brains rapidly and from Delta to Beta, and then back to Delta without enjoying the valuable Alpha and Theta states. The result is an agitated state of mind that hasn't been adequately relaxed.

The Alpha Advantage

Alpha production is an innate skill of our brains, but one consequence of the modern stressful lifestyle is that we forget how to produce Theta and Alpha brain waves. In doing so, we easily fall victim to anxiety and stress-related diseases. Anxiety and stress measurably reduce the strength of our immune systems. People who have more Alpha brain waves have less anxiety. Thus, having more Alpha waves could mean less anxiety and, correspondingly, stronger immune systems, which is good for everyone.

Creativity is another activity for which Alpha is helpful. Scientists have shown that highly creative people have different brain waves from normal and non-creative people. In order to have a creative inspiration, your brain needs to be able to generate a big burst of Alpha, mostly on the left side of the brain. The brains of creative people can generate these big Alpha bursts, and do so when they are faced with problems to solve. Normal and non-creative people do not produce Alpha waves when they are faced with problems, and so they cannot come up with creative ideas and solutions. Each time you have an insight or an inspiration, know that your brain just produced more Alpha waves than usual.

Peak performance is another activity for which Alpha is helpful. Recently, sports scientists have shown that increase of Alpha brain waves precede peak performance. One key difference between novice and elite athletes lies in their brain waves. Just before his best stroke, an accomplished cricketer will produce a burst of Alpha on the left side of his brain. Similarly, just before the final jump, an athlete will produce a burst of Alpha in the left-brain.

If you want to feel less stress and anxiety, you should increase the amount of your Alpha waves. This may also improve the strength of your immune systems, since stress weakens the immune systems. If you want to be more creative, you should learn how to increase the amount of your Alpha waves. Highly-creative people have more Alpha brain waves than non-creative people. If you want to have more peak performance in athletic activity, and in other areas of your life, you should learn how to increase the amount of your Alpha waves.

Most of the time we are using Beta Waves, which are associated with higher stress, and our day-to-day problem-solving. Relaxed and focused mental activity is associated with Alpha neural signalling. As anxious Beta neural activity decreases, clarity increases in mental activity. Learning occurs in an effortless manner. While experiencing Alpha, one realises an increased ability to solve problems; as a result, one quickly learns the advantages of existing in a clear perceptual state of mind. Sadly, most of us use the left (logical) side of our brain, which happens to be Beta-ruled.

The simple fact is that both Alpha and Theta waves are calming in nature, but the Theta waves, being very difficult to attain, remain elusive for most of us. But the Alpha can be attained, and that is what we must try to do. Whether you do it through meditation or prayers or whatever means is up to you.

A Quick Entry into the Alpha Mode

Although it may take a person quite some time to get into the Alpha brain waves, here is a simple method geared to give you quick result.

- Sit in a relaxed position – preferably on the ground in cross-legged position.
- Close your eyes and take three deep breaths.
- Turn the pupils upwards at an angle of about 22° and begin counting backwards from 100, in your mind.
- As you count 100-99-98-97-96-95... you will begin to feel calm.
- By the time you reach the count of 50, you would have attained the Alpha state.

Recap

- Stress is an adaptive response. It's the body's reaction to an event that is seen as emotionally disturbing, disquieting or threatening.

- Stress can cause emotional, behavioural and physical symptoms.
- A change of attitude, lifestyle and behaviour can lower stress levels.
- It is time to learn the art of breathing and the art of relaxing when you find you can't do them the natural way.
- The brain waves travel through varying cycles and are labelled into four categories – Alpha, Beta, Delta and Theta.
- Having more Alpha waves could mean less anxiety and, correspondingly, stronger immune systems.
- Highly creative people have more Alpha brain waves than non-creative people.

The Art of Relaxation

Close your eyes and try to picture the word 'relaxation'. What do you visualise?

Most of us would picture a retired life, an easy chair, sea waves, palm trees and birds. There could be some green coconuts or bikini clad girls around, depending on who is visualising. But the general picture remains the same.

What does the picture convey?

Just that we would all like to stop working and spend the rest of our lives with nature. The coconuts and the girls are the perks, I guess.

Wouldn't we all love living life as we picture it?

To most of us, relaxation is a state when the muscles in the body are at repose, the mind is unperturbed by disturbing thoughts and the soul is at peace. There is a peaceful and joyous feeling in the heart. In a heightened state of relaxation, a person is able to feel at the top of the world. He senses a joy in living and experiences euphoria. There is heightened awareness of the surroundings and a great sense of well-being that accompanies total repose.

Many people would like to think that they are relaxed while watching the television or having an alcoholic drink. Although they might get the feeling of stress ebbing away as they indulge in these activities, the stress promptly returns when the television is switched off or the drink finishes. The state of relaxation is experienced when the muscles are soft and pliant without any trace of tension and the mind is absolutely calm. The brain waves slow down to a state of emotional serenity and calmness. When the brain is totally relaxed, it attains the Alpha state with its rhythm slowing down to just 8–14 cycles per second.

The lack of relaxation can lead to many physical and emotional problems. For most people relaxation could mean just physical repose, but total relaxation is not just about the body being at rest. It is an all-encompassing state of repose where the body, mind and soul are in harmony, because resting one element without affecting the other is of little use. In other words, relaxation is the state when a person is at total rest. Any activity that differs from the normal routine of work or study can be relaxing. For instance, if you have a deskbound job for six days a week, an outdoor activity like hiking, nature trail or bungee jumping can be very relaxing. At the same time, if you have an outdoor job, taking a vacation by the seaside or in a hill station where you do nothing but loll under a tree can be highly relaxing. However, these will provide you physical relaxation and may not necessarily amount to mental relaxation. Nor would they guarantee rest for the soul or spirit.

Here are a couple of examples to illustrate the above statement:

Imagine that you've had a bad day at work. Your body is totally exhausted, the mind is absolutely restless and the soul disturbed. You return home, take a refreshing cold shower, carry a cup of coffee to the terrace and relax on your most comfortable chair. Are you relaxed? Of course, you must be relaxed physically. The cold shower, coffee and the cool air will definitely relax your body, and to some extent, your mind also. But the mind is still restless. Soon, you can't sit still or enjoy the comforts of your atmosphere. You remember a task – a deadline – and get restless. Reluctantly, you give up the efforts to rest and dash down to your study to catch up with the work. So, did you get the relaxation that you had attempted to grab? Most probably not! The restlessness of the mind didn't allow you to relax, despite the setting you created.

Now consider the same situation with a little difference. You are sitting on the terrace with the coffee, listening to soft, classical music – maybe humming along – as the cool breeze fans your tired limbs. Your mind is also at rest, lulled by the soothing notes of the music. The soul feels uplifted because there is harmony between the body and mind. You are totally relaxed and comfortable. There is no hurry and nothing breaks the rhythm of your repose. Compare this situation with the one given above. Don't you think that this is the ultimate relaxation – a fusion of the body, mind and soul for a common goal?

In another scenario, you've just returned from an exhausting day at work and want nothing more than a refreshing bath and a peaceful sleep. Just as you are about to enter the bathroom for the much-needed shower, your friend calls up and informs you that there is a party at his place and you are invited. Your inertia, exhaustion and irritation disappear in an instant. You rush with your bath, change into party togs and kick your motorcycle or rev up your car and speed towards the party venue.

Loud music, laughter and tinkle of glasses greet you as you arrive at your friend's party. Once there, you join the friends and begin dancing vigorously, all physical exhaustion forgotten in an instant. Would you say that you are relaxed? Of course, you are relaxed physically because you are enjoying yourself. But when the party breaks up at 2 a.m. you have a stiff headache, your entire body is aching and you find it difficult to catch up with sleep.

Next day, you wake up in a worse condition, your eyes bleary and red, your mind and body protesting against the excesses of the previous night. You won't call yourself relaxed, will you?

So, how does one relax in a holistic manner? It is a catch-22 situation. At certain times the very effort to relax makes a person tense. The word 'effort' then becomes a source of stress.

Holistic relaxation is not possible without all the three elements - body, mind and soul - coming together. Leisure is a word that has been wiped out of the dictionary of this generation. It is an alien word that puzzles and confuses them. At most, they are able to spend a couple of hours doing the things they like, but the rest of the day they are slogging to make more money, bound to their desks. A spell in the noisy pub in the evening and an attempt to unwind leads to more exhaustion than relaxation.

Stress and relaxation are two sides of the same coin, and both are necessary for a healthy life. When they are in balance, all is well, but if stress predominates, illness often develops - the possible consequences can range from headaches, anxiety and lethargy to heart attacks, ulcers or cancer.

Emotional frustration is more likely to cause stress-related disease, such as ulcers, than any type of physical work, though overwork accompanied by failure or lack of purpose can lead to exhaustion and even breakdown. However, the absence of work is no cure, and being excessively relaxed and indifferent to stress would mean missing out on all the wonderful feelings that add spice to life: euphoria, for example; excitement, heightened awareness of sounds, colour and smells, exhilaration, a sense of triumphing over the odds, and the heady scent of success. A well-adjusted approach to life's inherent pressures implies the juggling of all kinds of stress - both positive and negative - in order to achieve the balance we strive for.

Let me share a secret with you - most of the diseases are of the psychosomatic kind. What does that mean? Simply that the origin of these diseases lie in the mind.

You are what you think you are. It happened to me a few years back. I got caught in the web of ambition. I wanted to be the best journalist around, and that was not enough. I wanted to travel around the world and write about it. I also wanted to write books that made a difference to the lives around me. At the same time I was not willing to compromise on the family front. I wanted to be an ideal wife and mother too. I was full of dreams and the flight of my imagination knew no barriers.

So, what did I do? I began to work like a crazed woman. I worked through the day and sometimes through the night, trying to make the most of my time as though tomorrow would never arrive. Ultimately, I suffered from carpal tunnel syndrome that required that I keep off the computer keyboard. My body just refused to be mistreated. It gave up on me. And I realised that it was more important to streamline my ambitions. By-lines did not give me 'highs' any more. I slowed down and I am glad I did. Or I would have missed out on the beautiful things in life.

The 'WHAT' Syndrome

Most of us are caught in a similar trap all our life. We suffer from what I call the WHAT syndrome.

Psychosomatic diseases are not caused by any virus or bacteria. They are caused by 'what' syndrome. Before you begin to wonder what this WHAT is, let me explain that it is just an acronym of the words worries, hassles, anxiety and tension. Whether it is the common cold or bursting into skin rashes, most of the problems lie in the stressed minds. WHAT syndrome causes a weakening of the immune system, which in turn results in quick catching of infections.

But how can the WHAT syndrome cause diseases?

Most people think that our bodily health has nothing to do with the mind, which is absolutely wrong. Our thoughts and emotions have a major significance on the bodily health. Thoughts involve the entire body in a series of interrelated nerve impulses that centre in the brain. Psychologists say that it is the state of mind that manifests itself by a perceptible change in the body. Here is a perfect example of how the thought process can affect the body. When you are embarrassed, you blush and this process produces a dilation of the blood vessels in the face, which cause the redness on the face. When we are angry, the heart rate speeds up, the face reddens and the blood pressure seems to go up. Emotions cause enough physiological changes to warrant consideration.

As more and more of the WHAT syndrome occupies our lives, the number of psychosomatic diseases go up. The control of these illnesses lies in our hands. By getting the mind to relax, we can actually cure ourselves.

I meet a lot of people who refuse to believe that they are stressed. 'Oh I am totally relaxed. I don't do much, anyway,' some homemakers tell me. Believe me, you can be sitting at home, not doing much and yet getting stressed. Stress is not the prerogative of working people. It can attack anyone and everyone and it does. A funny thing about stress is that it can exhaust your body more than any other physical exercise. Haven't you noticed how drained you feel after a particularly stressful day even when you haven't done much physical work? Mental fatigue is more tiring than physical one.

How do you know that your body is relaxed?

When your body is relaxed, each muscle is in repose. Here is an easy test of relaxation.

- Lie down on your back with feet slightly apart and arms by your side.
- Breathe deeply and close your eyes.
- When you feel your body is totally relaxed, ask a friend to lift one of the arms or legs.
- Tell him to drop it suddenly.

- If the arm falls in a thud like a lifeless limb, without offering any resistance, you are totally relaxed.

RECAP

- Relaxation is a state of rest when the muscles in the body are loose and natural, the mind is unperturbed by disturbing thoughts and the soul is at peace.
- The lack of relaxation can lead to many physical and emotional problems.
- Pleasurable and relaxing activities help the body shed tension and promote health.
- Stress and relaxation are two sides of the same coin and both are necessary for a healthy life, but have to be kept in balance.
- Most of the diseases are of the psychosomatic nature. It is the WHAT syndrome that causes them.
- Worries, hassles, anxiety and tension make up the WHAT syndrome.

REJUVENATION

Have you ever noticed the leaves of a tree as they go through the different seasons? As autumn nears, the healthy, green leaves take on a brownish hue and finally fall from the tree. The tree looks totally forlorn, denuded and lonely. And then the spring season arrives. New leaves begin to appear on the tree, tender, delicate and beautiful. The tree begins to look beautiful, adorned with those tiny leaves. There is freshness, beauty and life once again. Our bodies also go through phases of tiredness, fatigue and exhaustion. The body cells die and need to be replaced. The exhausted systems need to be refreshed and energised. The damage caused by regular stress needs to be undone. Rejuvenation means regeneration, a new beginning, and a renewal of energy flow in the body.

To get rejuvenated, the body needs to recoup and rest. It has to go through a period of holistic relaxation before it can energise itself to face the multiple demands of modern living.

We are stressed because we have blocked the beauty of nature. Nature has the power to heal and rejuvenate. It has the ability to de-stress the mind. With the concrete jungles we have created, we have destroyed the natural jungles. No longer can we hear the birds; most people in cities can sight no other bird than the crow. Greenery is limited to the few parched and suffocated trees bereft of healthy leaves. Under such circumstances, is it a wonder that we are all highly stressed? We have to travel hundreds of kilometres for a tryst with nature.

Sometimes, when you are totally exhausted and weary, you take off for a vacation either at a hill station or near seashore. The clear blue water, silver sands, green swaying palm fronds bring a sense of joy and peace to you. You return to your job full of energy, vigour and enthusiasm because you have had your relaxation. You feel rejuvenated and refreshed. But, one can't keep taking off for vacations every time one is tired. So, we have to learn to relax within the constraints of modern living.

For a moment, chew on these facts: 60 trillion cells, more than 200 bones, at least 600 muscles, many systems, a complex network of blood vessels, nerves and a brain that is amazing – all constitute the human body. Every 72 hours your gut lining is completely replaced, every month your skin is renewed, every two years you manufacture a new skeleton and a new liver. That is an amazing amount of replacement work! Can you imagine the kind of renewal and recharging that is undertaken by the body on a constant basis? If you were to constantly abuse your body, giving it no respite, the process of renewal would go on but the quality could suffer. The body would have to struggle with the enhanced demands being made on it on a regular basis. Think about it. Would it not be easier for the body to go through the task of renewal if you slowed down for a while?

And this is just about the body. What about the mind? Well, that is an entirely different ball game, one that we will unravel gradually, throughout the book.

Many animals and plants hibernate during winter and wake up refreshed. Man doesn't do any such thing. In fact, many don't even take a holiday these days. So, how does he overcome exhaustion of the mind, body and soul? How does he recoup? Firstly, he has to learn to get rid of stress that pervades his body. Only when he has learnt the technique of stress release and relaxation can he go ahead and get recharged.

How does one, then, de-stress?

The effort should be to attain a state of mind when it is in a total state of relaxed alertness and there is an increase in the Alpha activity of the brain. This is the state when the body and emotions are balanced and the mind has attained a state of calmness and serenity.

Come to think of it, we all search for serenity constantly, yet we fail to find it most of the time. What do the words serenity and peace mean to you?

Perhaps you see yourself blissfully sitting by a stream in the woods or walking around a beautiful garden ablaze with flowers. Whatever the image, it likely depicts a place of silence. We often think of 'getting away from it all' to 'find' inner peace. Is it really necessary to get away from it all in order to find serenity? Does the act of running away bring peace? The truth is that it doesn't, because the moment you are back from your haven, you will find yourself right in the midst of the same turbulent world.

A few days back, there was a huge workshop held near my house. A famous yoga and spiritual guru had come to town. Huge banners and posters advertising the workshop were seen all around the town. The fee was steep, but the enthusiasm remained high as more than twenty thousand people lined up to get admitted to the five-day course.

There were yoga practices, discourses and talks through the five days, ending with a big bang. When the workshop ended, I asked a friend who had also enrolled for the course, 'Well, do you feel energised?'

He was in top form and spirit. 'It is a fantastic experience. After the yoga asanas my body feels so light and healthy. Even my paunch is beginning to disappear. I feel so happy and at peace with myself.'

I was happy for him.

I met him again, a couple of months later. He looked tired and stressed once again. 'What happened?' I asked.

'I am feeling totally dispirited and stressed,' he replied. 'The financial year is ending and work has piled up. I am working eighteen hours a day.'

'Aren't you continuing the yoga asanas and the spiritual exercises that you had learnt?'

'There is no time for all that. It just lasted for a few weeks.'

So, there he was, back to square one. His short assignation with serenity and fitness had ended already.

If you believe that serenity is something to be found... only by the lucky ones, rather than the fact that it is available to each and every one of us, you will keep looking for it somewhere 'out there'. In fact, serenity is always 'within', not something we win in some spiritual sweepstake. It is something we experience to varying degrees depending upon the decisions we make. We can choose to live our days in ways that illuminate and nurture this blissful state or we can follow the well-worn path of turmoil, chaos and conflict, hoping that we'll stumble on serenity one day.

Moreover, if you believe that serenity is inextricably related to 'getting away from it all', you limit yourself to regulated doses of running away to find peace. In a way, you actually push away the normal experience of inner peace. And by doing so, you are likely to relegate it to meditation sessions, yoga classes, weekend retreats, or perhaps a week at the beach. Such a concept makes us victims of daily stress and encourages an ineffective wait-for-vacation method of refuelling and rejuvenation.

Now think of another concept wherein you can visualise serenity as a precious jewel that lies within you... a treasure that you can unwrap whenever you want to, for a quick boost. Now, that kind of thinking promotes thoughts and actions that give rise to living in serenity on a daily basis.

You begin each day with a clear goal, before the day's business tosses you about like a straw in the wind. You stop during the day to take focusing breaks. You stop, breathe and remember what's important. You let go of all that is neither rewarding to you nor important to your mission. So, in a series of quick centring moments - perhaps in less time than it takes for a coffee break - you allow tranquillity to hug you. And with that hug comes the first spark of rejuvenation.

Relaxation and Rejuvenation

The word rejuvenation means rebirth, renewal, revival and resurrection. In a human body it is the re-energising of the tired and fatigued systems, weary cells and low-energy mind. Today, when we glance around, we see tired faces around us. People as young as 25–30 years of age looked jaded and faded, their eyes are lustre-less and their faces unsmiling. There is stress etched on each line of their faces.

Grey hair, associated with ageing, is now visible in the younger generation. Where have the smiles gone? The humour and lightness are slowly disappearing from our lives. Why has this happened?

Life on the fast track guarantees this phenomenon along with hundreds of bodily diseases. Success brings money, fame and laurels, but it can also bring with it stress, fatigue and ill health. In fact, most of the modern diseases are the gifts of a fast and successful life. This happens because most people do not know how to relax. Their idea of relaxation may be a peg of whiskey and loud, ear-shattering music or an escape to a beautiful place for the weekend.

Some of us would unwind at a spa for a weekend, trying to rejuvenate the weary cells of our body. Is that enough? Definitely not! The moment we are back to grind, the exhaustion and fatigue return. So, getting away for a weekend doesn't really do much good unless we learn to find a way to get away every weekend, which again is an impossibility for most of us. So what is the solution?

Within each of us is an infinite energy reservoir. Nature has gifted us with it, and all we need to do is to tap the reservoir of energy, to recharge ourselves.

Physical relaxation can be categorised into two parts – conscious muscular or motor relaxation and unconscious muscular relaxation. In the first kind, the aim is to withdraw consciousness and energy from the muscles at will. The complete absence of motion and tension from the muscles and limbs will bring about relaxation. If the body seems jelly-like, as if without bones or muscles, you have attained perfect muscular relaxation.

In the unconscious muscular relaxation, which is an imperfect method of relaxation, the limbs are moved about vigorously and then there is total stillness. This doesn't bring total relaxation but gives slight relief to the tensed-up muscles.

Recap

- Rejuvenations means regeneration, a new beginning and a renewal of energy flow in the body.
- To get rejuvenated the body needs to recoup and rest. It has to go through a period of holistic relaxation before it can energise itself to face the multiple demands of modern living.
- Nature has the power to heal and rejuvenate. It has the ability to de-stress the mind.

- The effort should be to attain a state of mind when it is in a total state of relaxed alertness and there is an increase in the alpha activity of the brain.
- Alpha state is the state when the body and emotions are balanced and the mind has attained a state of calmness and serenity.
- Serenity is always 'within', not something we win in some spiritual sweepstake.

The Need to Relax

Throughout the day, we are exposed to all kinds of action – actions of the physical nature, as well as the mental. Since every action, conscious or unconscious, uses stored energy, relaxation is necessary for good health and peace of mind. The body and mind experience true relaxation when little or no energy is consumed. It is Nature's way of recharging. It is true that there is very little physical action in the modern life as compared to the past; it is more of mental exhaustion that the present generation is experiencing. Deskbound jobs and ease of travelling have cut down the physical exercise factor. What is not realised is that even mental stress can bunch up the muscles and keep them taut through the day, leading to physical exhaustion.

Haven't you noticed how your jaws are clenched or the facial muscles tightened along with those in the shoulder and back, whenever you are stressed? These muscles can cause much discomfort and pain when they remain in the tense condition for a long time. Headaches, backaches and shoulder aches are just some of the manifestations of bunched-up and tense muscle groups.

Without proper relaxation the body and mind become overworked and inefficient. Exhausted body muscles need relaxation as much as the mind that is seized with anxiety and stress.

When my daughter was preparing for her Xth standard board exams, she drove us crazy with her stress levels. We knew that the stress could lead to her blanking out during the exams; she had suffered this problem earlier. Both my husband and I were worried because we didn't want her to blank out. For a week before the exam, we did everything we could think of to keep her away from stress. We told her that she had done as much as she could do, during the year, stressing over her books at the last moment was not likely to help.

We played cards with her, took her to movies, went out for dinners and did everything possible to keep her away from her books. She was annoyed at our efforts, but she knew that we were doing it for her good.

The exams went off without any hassles and when the results were announced, we were pleasantly surprised. She had scored 92 per cent average, with 96 per cent in maths – a subject that stressed her most. It is all about controlling the stress. The results are totally dependent on the state of mind.

The relentless exposure to daily, chronic anxiety is the most toxic form of stress. The body releases chemicals under high stress that can damage the immune system and increase the risk of all kinds of illnesses. Stress can harm neurons in the brain, causing memory problems, hamper sexual performance and lead to heart attacks. This should come as bad news for most people: stress can also make you fat. Digestive disturbances like flatulence, constipation, diarrhoea, acidity and stomach-aches are some of the other symptoms that can occur due to stress. Apart from all these physical problems, there are many psychosomatic and emotional manifestations that are caused by excessive stress.

Vitality, vim, vigour, energy – call it what you may – everything depends on how you recharge your batteries. Our body is like a rechargeable battery where the cells can be recharged by employing certain techniques. Before recharging, you have to relax and pause to take stock of your own bodily functions. Energising the cells requires patience, and you have to develop enough patience to take care of your own body. Nothing comes without effort, neither your success nor happiness, so how can the body be recharged without effort?

The recharging has to begin with relaxation and the first step in that direction is to bring in physical relaxation.

Physical Relaxation

Certain forms of exercise increase the body's energy, but this is futile if we continue to waste energy by constantly keeping the muscles in a state of readiness when there is no need to do so. Some people find they have trained their muscles to be so tense that they cannot relax them even at night, creating a constant energy drain.

Yoga asanas are a technique for retraining the muscles to be able to relax. People who practise asanas often find that they need less sleep and feel more rested. This is because, when they lie down, they quickly fall into a sound sleep. Deep sleep rejuvenates body and mind, but light sleep, or the dream state, actually uses energy.

Mental Relaxation

When the mind is constantly bombarded by stimuli, it becomes overloaded and exhausted. We may be unaware that we are doing it, but by thinking and worrying we are using up tremendous amounts of energy. The tension put on the mind by worries, whether real or imagined, can use more energy than physical work.

When worries get out of hand, energy resources are strained. Mental fatigue sets in, often resulting in wear and tear on the physical body as well. It is important to set aside some time each day for the mind to unwind and recoup its energies.

Mental relaxation would mean the ability to free the mind from nagging worries, fears, greed and disturbing thoughts. It should mean the moving away from negative thoughts and emotions to the positive ones.

Whenever you experience mental tension, try breathing slowly and rhythmically for a few minutes while you concentrate on the breath. Yogic breathing exercises may take conscious effort, but develop your ability to calm the mind using your own thought power. This leads to an experience of inner peace, with physical relaxation following the mental relaxation.

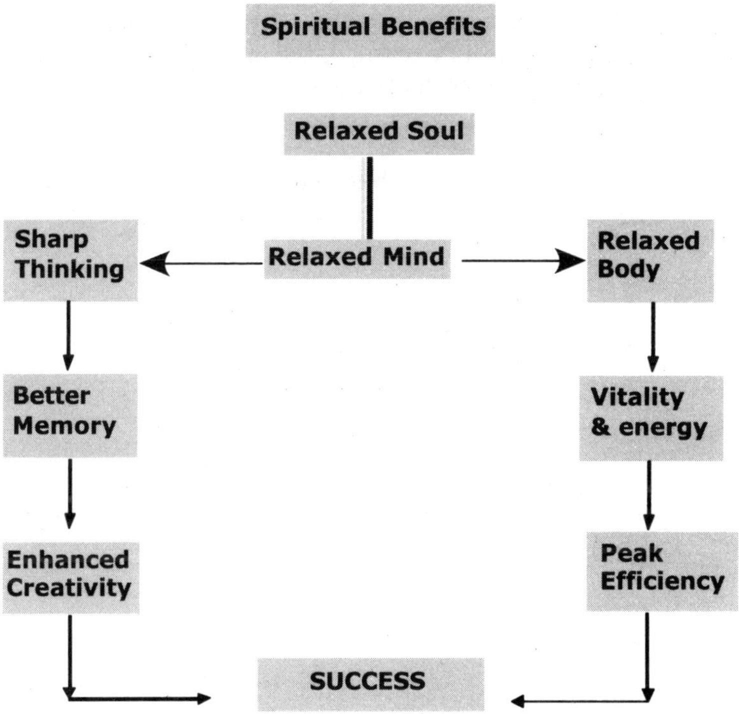

Spiritual Relaxation

Complete mental and physical relaxation comes only with an inner tuning to a higher source. As long as we identify with this body and mind, we all think we can rely on no one but ourselves. There will always be tension and worries about the future. Tuning to the divine source brings the realisation that all happiness comes from within. Yoga gives the techniques for this inner tuning, enabling us to break down the boundaries that separate us from each other, and from our own inner selves.

RECAP

- When you are exhausted and stressed, everything seems unexciting and difficult. Neither the home nor office feels good.
- The feel-good factor comes with relaxation.
- Without relaxation there can be no rejuvenation.
- The relentless exposure to daily, chronic anxiety is the most toxic form of stress.
- Your vitality and energy levels depend on how you recharge your batteries.
- The body releases chemicals under high stress that can damage the immune system and increase the risk of all kinds of illnesses. Stress can harm neurons in the brain, causing memory problems, hamper sexual performance and lead to heart attacks.
- The lack of relaxation can lead to many physical and emotional problems.
- Rejuvenation cannot take place until the body cells have relaxed.
- Relaxation that is holistic promotes rejuvenation; holistic relaxation includes the mind, body and spirit.
- Complete mental and physical relaxation comes only with an inner tuning to a higher source.
- Rejuvenation increases efficiency. It brings freshness, energy and happiness.

HOLISTIC RELAXATION

Can a person who is mentally tired remain physically relaxed? Is it possible for a physically exhausted person to remain mentally agile?

The answer to both the questions is 'NO'. Just as it is not possible for a physically exhausted person to remain mentally alert, it is not feasible for a mentally exhausted person to be brimming with physical energy. This is where the word holistic comes into the picture. For complete relaxation it is necessary to be mentally, physically and emotionally relaxed.

The term 'holistic' is increasingly being used in all kinds of healing systems. Whether it is health, diet or relaxation, a holistic approach has to be followed in order to attain the maximum benefit. The holistic approach requires a complete balance and harmony between the three aspects of our life – physical, mental and spiritual. There is a lot of mention nowadays about work and lifestyle balance.

What does a balanced life look like to you? Balance can be described as 'harmony and proportion'. Balance is about feeling connected to ourselves and enjoying a sense of rhythm and flow between mind, body and spirit. It's about being flexible – having awareness about what's going on within the three aspects, at any given time, and equally important, having the ability to respond to the messages that you're receiving, recognising the distress signs sent by any of the aspects and striving to stabilise and return to harmony.

If you think about it, when we balance on something, we're always moving as we seek to remain in equilibrium. Think of the tightrope walker, and how he adjusts his position on the rope continuously in order to remain upright. Likewise, in nature, the universe is always seeking equilibrium. Think of our bodies and homeostasis, the means by which the internal systems of the body (e.g. blood pressure, body temperature) are maintained, despite possibly extreme variations in external conditions; also the way in which as cells die in a healthy person they are replaced by exactly the same number. We don't have to think about these bodily processes, but constant awareness of our thoughts is required to create mental and physical balance. For a holistic approach and harmony between the body, mind and spirit, we have to make consistent and sincere effort.

Whenever one of the aspects of our life is out of harmony, the others are likely to suffer. If we feel mentally stressed, the physical ailments make their appearance with an amazing alacrity. Similarly, if the body is exhausted, the mind also suffers. A tired body does not allow a quick decision-making or deep concentration. It demands rest and forces the mind to rest, too.

When is the soul exhausted? I would think that a spirit that has to deal with a host of negative thoughts and guilt would feel tired and spent. To cleanse the soul is to refresh and relax. It is to feel like a child – innocent and guileless. We are all born with a soul that is pure and shining. Over a period of years, we manage to wrap it with sheets of negativity and guilt, and then one day, we begin to feel that we can no longer recognise the purity of our soul. It becomes tarnished and tired beyond recognition.

The little acts of cheating and the small instances of lies that we heaped on it through our lives have suddenly taken on immense dimensions. The sheets of corruption wrapping it have thickened and we begin to feel the burden of it all. Now, it is time for a cleansing act, we decide, because the repercussions have begun to show on our minds and bodies as well. The little body aches have magnified into arthritic pains, migraines and other problems. No longer can we remain immune to the threats of our troubled soul. It needs purification through relaxation, and slowly we begin to discover the need to cleanse the layers of dirt that have accumulated over it. Like the multiple skins of the onion, the layers of wrongdoings have to be peeled, one by one. As we progress with the act of peeling, we discover our new self and experience a joyous and wondrous feeling of exultation.

We realise that we have tuned into the realm of true happiness. We experience the calmness of our undisturbed soul. It is no longer restless or fretful. It is at peace with the world and in true harmony with our mind and body. This is the ultimate state of relaxation.

Anand Rao was suffering from a strange ailment. Occasionally, his skin would burst into angry rashes accompanied by unbearable itching. He consulted several skin specialists and faithfully applied the ointments and lotions prescribed by them. He swallowed the pills they gave him, but the rashes continued to trouble him. On the recommendations of a friend, he attended one of the meditation courses run by a known spiritual guru in town. What followed was an amazing phenomenon. Three days down the workshop, during a session when the participants were to recall the people they had not forgiven and perform the act of forgiving. Anand recalled his estranged wife and forgave her for the wrongs he considered had been done to him. He felt cleansed after the session and confessed to his teacher about the change. The skin problem he had been suffering from a long time disappeared. Later, the teacher informed him that the ailment was a manifestation of the resentment he had harboured for so many years.

Sometimes the physical ailments are just a reflection of the negative emotions that are stored in our hearts. Getting rid of them acts as a spring-cleaning of the physical self.

Yin and Yang

The idea of harmony and balance are the basis of yin and yang. The belief that the opposing, but complementary forces of yin and yang govern each person is central to all Chinese thought because it is believed to affect everything in the universe, including us.

Traditionally, yin is dark, passive, feminine, cold and negative; yang is light, active, male, warm and positive. Modern therapists would simply say that there are two sides to everything – happy and sad, tired and energetic, cold and hot.

Yin and yang are the opposites that make the whole, they cannot exist without each other and nothing is ever completely one or the other; there are varying degrees of each within everything and everybody. The body, mind and emotions are all subjects to the influences of yin and yang. When the two opposing forces are in balance, we feel good, but if one force dominates the other, it brings about an imbalance that can result in ill health.

When we connect with our inner self, we learn that a heightened appreciation of our senses can prove invaluable for a more peaceful state of mind. For example, through some forms of touch our body can release its natural painkillers or balance our 'chi', as the Chinese call it, 'ki' as per the Japanese, or 'prana' energy according to traditional Indian practices. Sound therapy, in the form of soothing music, can help to slow our brainwaves to induce a profound sense of relaxation. The vital energy, prana, keeps the body healthy. Greeks called it 'Pneuma', Polynesians 'Mana', and in Hebrew it is known as 'Ruah', the breath of life. We constantly drain our life energy by thoughts, actions and emotions, and need to constantly replenish the vital energy through various means like meditation, pranic breathing, etc.

Recap

- Holistic relaxation requires a complete balance and harmony between the physical, mental and spiritual aspects of our life.
- Yin and yang are the opposites that make the whole; they cannot exist without each other. The body, mind and emotions are all subjects to the influences of yin and yang.
- In the Chinese philosophy, inner harmony relies on a healthy, balanced and unobstructed flow of chi.

- Chi is an invisible, intangible flow of energy.
- When chi flows freely though the meridians, the body is balanced and healthy, but if the energy becomes blocked, stagnated or weakened, it can result in physical, mental or emotional ill health.

CHAPTER TWO

Physical Relaxation

There is hardly anyone who does not know the meaning of physical tiredness. Whether we are busy executives, students or homemakers, we all suffer from physical exhaustion at some time or the other. Even sitting at the desk and working on the computer can bring about exhaustion. Commuting to work, driving, studying for long hours can bring fatigue and muscular exhaustion of some kind or the other. Our body is an amazing and complex creation. Can you imagine that 300 million cells die in the body every minute, but the number of cells remains almost constant throughout our life because the new cells replace the dead ones at once? All these cells are constantly moving, pulsating and dividing. The adult body has 206 bones and more than 600 muscles in it. Each of the muscles has a specialised function, many of them work continually even when we sleep. There are almost 30 muscles attached to the bones of the skull and their job is to give our face expression. Imagine, all those thirty muscles coming to work even if you smile or grimace. That's a lot of work!

The body has a lot of hard work to do, just to cope with the bodily functions. And when you make it work beyond its capacity, it protests by making you ache.

The Importance of Physical Relaxation

When the body is tired, the mind becomes stagnant and dull. Often, when you are dead tired, you don't want to spend time solving a problem; all you want to do is to sleep or find some way to relax. It is said that a healthy mind resides in a healthy body. I will twist that saying slightly to read – an active and intelligent mind resides in a relaxed and rejuvenated body. When the mind and body are tired and exhausted, can the spirit remain unaffected? Of course not! It becomes jaded and shattered. You feel like a deflated balloon that refuses to rise up, no matter how strong the wind is. Your spirit, too, refuses to soar like the deflated balloon.

So what do you do?

You have to relax and recoup. And how does one begin? One begins with the body, naturally. A refreshed body will revitalise the mind and in turn cause the spirit to soar.

Basic Relaxation Technique

We store our tension in various muscle groups. For some, it could be the muscles in the shoulder and neck region, while for others it could well be the back muscles. This basic relaxation technique is geared to reduce accumulated stress in the body, by progressively contracting and relaxing the muscle groups that store tension.

While it is essential that our muscles maintain a certain amount of tension to support posture and movement, it is when our bodies have to move unnaturally or under stress that the result can be extra, unnecessary tension in certain muscles – for example, in neck and shoulders. This is the major reason for stress-headaches, aches and pains, and general tiredness. And so the vicious circle is established.

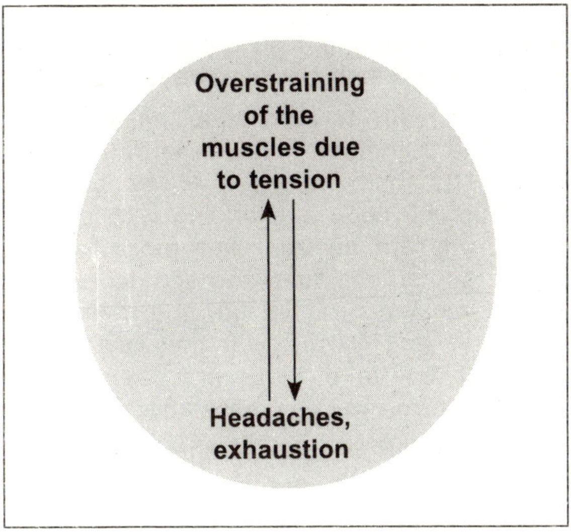

The Vicious Circle

To break out of this circle we need to know how to release excess tension from the muscles – this is the first step in relaxation, and is used in all the various techniques. Most of the time we tend to concentrate on what is happening in the outside world around us, but the first rule of relaxation is to bring that focus back inside ourselves. This helps us to become sensitive to the tensions within our bodies, and then we can begin to relieve them.

A Simple Technique to Get You Started

1. Wear loose and comfortable clothes. Lie down in a quiet and dark room, preferably using a mat on the floor. Place a pillow or cushion under your head and knees. Either let your hands and arms rest by your side or gently upon your stomach, whichever feels the most comfortable.

2. Check that you feel really comfortable. If necessary, use more pillows – perhaps under your feet and forearms. Start the technique only when you are certain of your comfort because the slightest sense of discomfort can ruin the technique.
3. Relax and let your mind go blank. Take a couple of deep breaths and sigh the air away.
4. Now you are ready to start reducing tension in your muscles. The technique involves letting go of all the muscles in the body, starting at the toes, working gradually up the body and ending with the face. To begin, concentrate on your left foot. Tense all the muscles – curling the toes and scrunching the foot. Hold for a few seconds. Let go, and make them feel floppy, heavy and warm, as if they are sinking into the pillow. It may take a little practice to perfect this technique, but you will get there after a while.
5. Move onto the calf muscles on the left leg. Tense the muscles, hold and let go. Feel the heaviness and warmth of the leg and foot.
6. Apply the same technique on the left thigh. Concentrate on the left leg – does it feel heavy, warm, and relaxed. Is it sinking into the floor or bed? If the answers are 'no', tense the whole leg, hold it in tension until it feels difficult to hold the position any longer, then let go completely.
7. Repeat the same process with the right leg.
8. When both legs feel heavy and numb, continue moving up the body. Clench your buttocks tightly and let go; pull in your stomach muscles, hold tight, relax; let them fall back towards the spine into the floor or bed. Feel the warmth spreading up your body.
9. Breathe deeply and evenly a few times, then sigh the breath away; imagine you are sighing all the tension out of your body.
10. Move on to your left hand, squeeze your hand into a fist, hold tight and let go. Tighten the muscles in the

arm and then let them flop. Continue with your right arm. Repeat if the arms are not relaxed and heavy. They should feel numb and impossible to move.

11. Hunch your shoulders up towards your ears, hold, let go; let them sink into the floor. It may be necessary to repeat this movement a few times as we hold a lot of tension in our shoulders. Pull the shoulders up towards the ceiling and let them flop back into the ground. Repeat a couple of times.
12. Rock your head gently from side to side in order to loosen the neck. Feel the total relaxation of the body and breathe deeply a few times. Relax, feel the warmth and quiet.
13. The face is the most difficult part of the body to relax; yawn widely with an open mouth, let go; purse the lips out in a pout, then relax; frown fiercely, let go; move the scalp by raising the eyebrows, then relax.
14. By now your whole body should feel relaxed. Breathe evenly in and out, saying to yourself with each breath that you feel more and more relaxed, peaceful and warm.
15. Rest for around 15 minutes. Do not jump up and start racing around. Let yourself come slowly and gently.
16. Stretch and give yourself a shake before joining the rat race once again.

Relaxation Checklist

Once you have mastered the basic relaxation techniques, you can apply them almost anywhere. It is important, though, to cultivate an awareness of how your body feels throughout the day, so that you can learn to recognise the difference between normal and unnatural amounts of tension. Once you begin to notice when and where you tense up, you can pinpoint your exercises to relax those muscle groups that are affected.

1. Don't leap out of bed in the morning late, with too much to do before you start the day. Set the alarm just 5 minute earlier to give yourself time to relax.
2. Plan to have time for yourself at home – for example, when the children are at school, or playing peacefully. Let the family know that certain times of the day are 'your time' – then lie down or sink into a chair and empty your mind of all household and work problems. Concentrate on how your body feels and note areas of tension; then use the relaxation technique.
3. Watch out for tension in your shoulders and arms when driving a car. Are you gripping the steering wheel, sitting bolt upright and frowning? At traffic lights or in a traffic jam, take a few seconds to concentrate on yourself; hunch the shoulders up, then let them flop down; slacken your grip on the steering wheel; relax back into your seat and feel the tension leave your body. Breathe slowly and deeply – it is difficult to become angry and frustrated while you are doing this.

A Simple Way to Relax the Entire Body Quickly

- Tense all the body parts (there are 20 of them), feet to neck.
- Clench the fists and then quickly relax.
- Exhale and keep still.
- Repeat the process all over the body and do it twice.
- The body should feel like a jellyfish when you have finished.

RECAP

- When the mind and body are tired and exhausted, you feel like a deflated balloon that refuses to rise up, no matter how strong the wind is. Your spirit too refuses to soar.

- A refreshed body revitalises the mind. That, in turn, causes the spirit to soar.
- A basic relaxation routine should relax the taut muscles, refresh the mind and bring solace to the soul.

Stretch the Stress Away

Have you noticed the most normal reaction to stress? If you are a keen observer, you will notice that one of the quickest responses your body has to stress is increased muscle tension and contraction. The muscles of our body tense up into rigid balls of tautness, which can leave us absolutely fatigued by the end of the day. The physiological reason for this muscular activity is to prepare us for fight or flight but, in reality, the resolution of modern day stresses and problems require neither fight nor flight. When muscle tension continues for long periods without physical release, a low, or even moderate, level of chronic pain may develop, especially in the shoulders, neck and lower back.

Stretching the affected muscles is the best way to combat the tightness in them. To break the contraction cycle and relax these muscle areas, stretch each of them at least ten or more times, each day.

Here are a few crucial combat techniques geared to relax the most affected muscles of the body.

Head Roll

1. Drop your head to extend your right ear toward your right shoulder. Hold this position 10 to 20 seconds.
2. From this position, roll your head forward to touch your chin to your chest. Hold this position 10 to 20 seconds.

3. Roll your head to the left to extend your left ear toward your left shoulder. Hold this position 10 to 20 seconds.
4. Now, roll your head forward again to touch your chin to your chest. Hold this position 10 to 20 seconds.
5. Lastly, lift your head to centre on top of your shoulders. Repeat a few times.
6. Sit on the knees, knees touching each other, heels together, soles facing upwards.
7. Bend forward. Rest the forehead on the ground. Place the palms on either side of the head.
8. Move forward and backward with your feet as the pivot.
9. Inhale while moving forward. Exhale while coming back. Repeat at least 5 times.

Tiger-stretch

1. Position yourself on your fours.
2. Rest on the palms and the knees. Do not bend the elbow joint. Keep your heels apart.
3. Bring the head inwards flexing the spine up while exhaling fast through the mouth. The spine should be in a convex curve.
4. While inhaling and raising the hand up, arch the spine towards the floor. The spine is now in a concave shape upwards.
5. Repeat and increase the speed gradually.
6. Lie down on the abdomen, rest the chest on the ground and relax completely.
7. If all the movements are done slowly, synchronising with slow and deep breathing, it is known as Tiger breathing.
8. This exercise stretches the spine.

Upper Back Stretch

1. Stand in open doorway.
2. Grab onto the back of the doorframe with both your right and left hands.
3. Holding on securely, lean forward until you feel the stretch across your chest.
4. Hold the stretch 20 to 30 seconds.

Lower Back Stretch

1. Lie down on a firm surface on your back. Keep one leg straight for support.
2. Bend the other knee and place both hands behind it. (Do not place hands over the kneecap. Clasp hands behind the knee.)
3. Gently pull the bent knee up toward your chest, letting its lower leg relax.
4. Relax your head back onto the floor. Hold this stretch with firm, consistent pressure by the supporting hands for 20 to 30 seconds.
5. The muscles in your lower back should feel a stretch but no pain. If you feel pain, reduce the amount of stretch until you are comfortable again. Repeat this stretch on the other side.

RECAP

- Stress causes the muscles of our body to tense up into rigid balls of tautness, which can leave us absolutely fatigued by the end of the day.
- To relax the body, it is necessary to relax the muscles that have grown taut. The most affected muscles are those of the neck, shoulders, and back.
- Stretching the affected muscles is the best method to relax them.

Progressive Muscle Relaxation

Progressive Muscle Relaxation (PMR) is one of the most simple and easy to learn techniques for physical relaxation. Originally developed by Jacobson in 1939, this procedure has found a horde of followers the world over.

The PMR procedure is the simplest technique that one can do anywhere, anytime with great results. It works much like the basic relaxation technique, with a little difference. It simply involves the relaxation of body's muscles through a two-step process. The first step is to deliberately apply tension to certain muscle groups, and then discontinue the tension while turning the attention to notice how the muscles relax as the tension flows away. The bonus is the mental calmness that comes with physical relaxation.

A word of caution for people who have a history of serious injuries, muscle spasms or back problems – please consult your doctor before trying out PMR because the deliberate muscle-tensing could aggravate these problems.

How to do PMR – before you begin the procedure, a little knowledge about the muscle groups will help greatly. Since the workout must follow a certain order, we have to begin from the feet and move upwards. The sequences of the different muscle groups that will come into play are:

- Right foot
- Right lower leg and foot
- Entire right leg
- Left foot
- Left lower leg and foot
- Entire left leg
- Right hand
- Right forearm and hand
- Entire right arm

- Left hand
- Left forearm and hand
- Entire left arm
- Abdomen
- Chest
- Neck and shoulders
- Face

Step One - Building up the Tension

To begin PMR, focus your mind on the muscle group; for example, your right hand. Then inhale and simply squeeze the muscles as hard as you can for about 8 seconds; this would involve making a tight fist with your hand.

Most beginners usually make the mistake of allowing muscles other than the intended group to tense as well; in the example, this would be tensing muscles in your right arm and shoulder, not just in your right hand. With practice, you will be able to differentiate the specific muscles. For the moment, however, just do the best you can.

PMR isn't just about tension and relaxation – it is also about muscle discernment.

Remember, no part of the body is an isolated unit. The muscles of the hand, for example, do have connections in the forearm, so when you tense your hand, there will always be some small tension occurring in the forearm. It's important to really feel the tension. Done properly, the tension procedure will cause the muscles to begin shaking slightly, and you will feel some pain.

The watchwords should be – gentle and deliberate. Be careful not to hurt yourself. Mild pain is all right, but if it pains too much, you are not doing it right. Contracting the muscles in your feet and your back especially can cause serious problems if not done carefully.

Step Two - Releasing the Tension

This is the best part because it is really pleasurable. After the 8 seconds of contracting the muscles, quickly and suddenly let go. Let all the tightness and pain flow out of the muscles as you exhale simultaneously. It is beneficial to visualise tightness and pain flowing out of your hand through your fingertips as you exhale. Feel the muscles relax and become loose and limp, tension flowing away like water out of a tap. Turn your focus on the difference between tension and relaxation.

Stay relaxed for about 15 seconds, and then repeat the tension–relaxation cycle. You are likely to notice more sensations the second time.

Once you understand the muscle groups and the tension–relaxation procedure, then you are ready to begin the full PMR training. Simply follow the list of muscle groups in the sequence given and work through your entire body. Practise twice a day for a week. Spend extra time, if necessary, until you can achieve a deep sense of physical relaxation.

A Few Guidelines

- Always practise full PMR in a quiet place, alone, with no electronic distractions, not even background music.
- Remove your shoes and wear loose clothing.
- Avoid eating, smoking or drinking. It's best to practise before a meal rather than after, for the sake of your digestive processes.
- Never do the PMR after using any intoxicants.
- Sit in a comfortable chair if possible. You may practise lying down, but this increases the likelihood of falling asleep.
- If you practise in bed at night, plan on falling asleep before you complete your cycle. Therefore, consider a practice session at night in bed in addition to your basic practice.

- When you finish a session, relax with your eyes closed for a few seconds, and then get up slowly. Standing up suddenly can make you feel faint due to orthostatic hypotension – a sudden drop in blood pressure. Some people like to count backwards from 5 to 1, timed to slow, deep breathing along with suggestive words like supremely calm, fully alert, feeling good, etc.

RECAP

- PMR (Progressive Muscle Relaxation) is a powerful muscle relaxation technique that is increasingly being used by therapists to de-stress bunched up muscles.
- It is done in two steps. In the first step, the muscles are contracted and in the next one, they are relaxed.
- When you practise the procedure repetitively, you learn to differentiate between the feelings of a tensed muscle and a completely relaxed muscle. You can, then, induce physical muscular relaxation at the first signs of the tension that accompanies anxiety.
- With physical relaxation comes mental calmness, in any situation.
- It is important to know about the specific muscle groups that need to be contracted at a given moment.
- It is also important to distinguish between the feelings of tension and relaxations of the muscles.
- Once the technique has been learnt, a shorter version can be practised on a daily basis.
- PMR results in relaxation of the body and calmness of the mind.

Slumber Power

Miss Dinshaw has been struggling with insomnia for the past two years. She is a thirty-year-old bank employee. She suffers from the chronic-worrier syndrome. A vicious cycle haunts her – worries cause insomnia, and the insomnia causes more worries. So how does she get out of this terrible circle of problems?

Arun Thakkar, 45, a stock exchange broker, is seized with sleepless nights, which are causing enough problems for him to seek the help of his doctor. Six months and many sleeping pills later, he still remains a sleepless man. His problems are lofty ambitions and financial worries.

I remember, sometime back, I was watching an interview of the yesterday's star Nadira. In the interview, she spoke about her insomnia and how big a torture it is to lie awake in the bed, waiting for the morning to arrive while the entire world is sleeping. Tossing and turning through the night, night after night, was a nightmare. She spoke about how it was driving her crazy.

In a recent interview, talk-show hostess and yesteryear star, Simi Garewal admitted that she suffers from sleep problem and keeps awake till 5 am. She attributed it to her overactive mind.

These are not isolated cases; a walk into a doctor's clinic will tell you that more people are seeing physicians for sleepless nights and insomnia than ever before. It would seem that a relaxing slumber is getting more and more difficult for most people to enjoy. With the world around us becoming noisier, worrisome and unhealthy, is it a wonder that sleep is the causality? Yet, it is the most essential thing in life. You may survive without food for more than a fortnight but deprivation of sleep for two weeks could drive you insane or even kill you.

Studies have thrown up some unbelievable facts. Scientists have discovered a relationship between the quantity and quality of one's sleep and many health problems. For example, did you know that insufficient sleep affects growth hormone secretion that is linked to obesity? Unbelievable but true! As the amount of hormone secretion decreases, the chances for weight gain increase.

Blood pressure usually falls during the sleep cycle, but interrupted sleep can lead to hypertension and cardiovascular problems.

Research has also shown that insufficient sleep impairs the body's ability to use insulin, which can lead to the onset of diabetes. More and more scientific studies are showing correlations between poor and insufficient sleep and disease.

Lack of sleep can slow down reflexes and dull the mind. A few days of sleep deprivation can cause impaired reflex action and hamper concentration.

Sound sleep also keeps the heart healthy and stems the release of catecholamines, a hormone released by the parasympathetic nervous system during our waking hours, which results in slowing down the heart rate and causes relaxation in the blood vessels.

Lack of sleep impairs the immune system and lowers our ability to fight diseases. There is no doubt about the healing powers of sleep. Latest research has proved that we need at least seven to nine hours of deep sleep to keep healthy.

While we rest and sleep, our body goes through a period of intense physiological and mental activity. Human beings cannot survive without a regular period of sleep – in fact, no living beings can. Besides, we need to sleep at regular intervals – it is not as useful to the body to have 5 hours of sleep one night and 12 hours the next. The body has a meticulous working system that operates on a 24-hour basis and finds it difficult to adjust to abnormal variations. The working of the body clock, which is based on the movement of the earth round the sun and the consequent periods of light and dark, is known as the 'circadian rhythm'.

The body takes many days, even weeks, to get out of the circadian rhythm, and during that time physical co-ordination, alertness and other manifestations of mental ability function less effectively. This is one of the reasons why the productivity levels of the workers on a night shift could be less than those of workers on a day shift. Anyone who has travelled between continents by jet will know how difficult it is to adjust to a new time scale. The jet lag that occurs leaves the person feeling muddled and fuzzy and can take several hours of sleep to help him recover.

In order to make decisive and logical judgements and carry on other thinking processes, the brain needs regular doses of sleep. Experiments have shown that sleeplessness does not impair physical activity but it definitely impairs concentration. People become increasingly vague the longer they go without sleep, eventually suffering from hallucinations - literally dreaming with their eyes open.

When asleep, the body and brain are not completely dead to the world or unconscious. The essential 'life support systems' of the heart, digestion, cell repair and replacement continue happening even during our sleep. The senses also continue to be active to a certain degree - when an alarm clock rings, a part of your head registers the sounds of the bell and responds to the stimulus, sometimes dragging you unwillingly from sleep. Another part of the brain allows us to ignore regular noises, like the traffic outside or the whirring of a fan or an air-conditioner. In this way, even while asleep, the brain apparently selects the intake of stimuli and lets us respond to some, but not to all.

The Importance of Sleep

Anyone who sleeps well will wake up energised. While some people may argue that they can get away with little sleep, others may insist on grabbing a full eight hours of sleep before they can perform at their peak efficiency. Why is it important to sleep? Researchers have found that sleep is as essential to the body as nourishment.

Is there any substance to the belief that sleep before midnight is more effective than the sleep after the witching hour?

Although people tend to think that deeper sleep comes late in the night, there is enough evidence to reveal that the brain gets the most refreshing and beneficial sleep in the earlier cycles of the sleep period. So, perhaps there is some truth in the saying that sleep before midnight is better than sleep in the early hours - if a person's usual time for going to bed is about 10 pm. But, obviously, if someone is accustomed to sleeping from midnight until 10 am, he will draw the greatest benefit from his sleep between midnight and 2 am. In the same way, you do not necessarily need double sleep to recuperate from a very late night. In such cases, the body simply makes up the lost resting time by going into longer periods of big-wave sleep on the following night. Most people find that a normal period of sleep, which is about 7–8 hours, is enough to repair the damage of a late-night party - although it does not take into account other bad effects that might also be present - like alcohol.

Relaxing Sleep

Although most of us know the benefits of deep sleep, some may not be able to enjoy it due to some reason or the other. Miss Dinshaw claims that she doesn't sleep a wink through the night. Sometimes the claim is an exaggeration, but at other times it is a genuine case of insomnia, which can be a very exasperating experience.

Those who know what a torture it is to remain awake, tossing through the night, unable to grab the resting slumber, realise that the causes of many ailments is their inability to sleep. Most of us know the feeling. You want to sleep, but you can't sleep. Some nights it seems you never drop off at all. And most of us know the name of this dreaded affliction - insomnia.

While some people suffer from difficulty in falling asleep (initial insomnia); others wake up repeatedly at night (middle insomnia); or they are unable to go back to sleep after they wake up earlier than usual in the morning (late insomnia). Some insomniacs resort to taking medication to sleep, which can start off a vicious and unbreakable cycle of drug dependency. Persistent efforts to battle insomnia through alternative methods often works quite efficiently, but most insomniacs give up the effort due to lack of patience.

Sleepless Nights

Causes: The causes are many and varied: stress, shift work, caffeine, alcohol abuse and disrupted sleep schedules. With chronic insomnia, usually sleeplessness is a symptom rather than the actual problem. Stress, physical ailments or depression disrupt sleep. Chronic stress is the commonest cause of insomnia, as is depression. The sufferer lies awake worrying instead of dropping off to sleep. This can lead to even deeper depression, to more stress and to physical ailments like stomach ulcers.

Cures: If you suffer from short-term insomnia, there are many methods to help alleviate the problem. These range from warm baths to warm milk, herbal tea or other herbal remedies to the various relaxation techniques like yoga, visualisation and meditation. Daytime exercise is usually beneficial. Heavy meals or sugar-laden treats late in the evening can cause stomach distress and sleeplessness. Don't drink coffee or smoke prior to bedtime, as caffeine and nicotine are stimulants. Neither is it wise to use alcohol to promote sleep. This can lead to serious problems. The use of alcohol disrupts normal sleep patterns and REM sleep. Also, as alcohol is a drug and addictive, you may become dependent on it to put you to sleep.

If none of these methods works for you, or if you suspect you may be suffering from chronic insomnia, seek medical advice. A doctor can search for underlying causes or prescribe medication. Before going to your doctor, it's a good idea to keep a sleep diary for a few weeks. Keep a notebook by the bed and mark down the hours when you are awake. This may help you detect your sleep patterns and indicate how many hours of sleep you're really getting.

One thing I've discovered when plagued by occasional bouts of insomnia is that fighting it solves little. Lying in bed tossing, turning, trying to force those eyes to stay closed only aggravates the problem.

What can you do? Get up and find some chores that keep you from worrying about your insomnia. Sometimes watching TV or reading will make you sleepy. If you are able, and if you live in a safe area, a night-time walk may work for you.

Here are some simple methods that can help you grab restful sleep.

Clockwork: Maintain a regular bed-and-wake time schedule including weekends. Our sleep-wake cycle is regulated by a 'circadian clock' in our brain. It also takes care of the body's need to balance both sleep time and wake time. A regular waking time in the morning strengthens the circadian function and can help you sleep at night. That is also why it is important to keep a regularbedtime and wake-time, even on the weekends when there is the temptation to sleep in.

Relaxing Routine: Establish a regular, relaxing bedtime routine such as soaking in a hot bath or hot tub and then reading a book or listening to soothing music. A relaxing, routine activity right before bedtime conducted away from bright light helps separate your sleep time from activities that can cause excitement, stress or anxiety which can make it more difficult to fall asleep, get sound and deep sleep or remain asleep. Avoid arousing activities before bedtime like working, exercising, engaging in competitive games or family problem-solving. Some people swear by the efficacy of a luxurious soak in a bathtub filled with warm water, for a restful sleep. A few drops of essential oils like lavender, rose, frankincense, added in the bath water work wonders by lulling and sedating the mind. If you are unable to avoid tension and stress, it may be helpful to learn relaxation therapy from a trained professional. Finally, avoid exposure to bright lights before bedtime because they signal to the neurons that help control the sleep–wake cycle that it is time to awaken, not to sleep. For the same reason, those who visit discotheques and dance under the flashing strobe lights may find sleep eluding them for long hours.

Keep It Cool: Create a sleep-conducive environment that is dark, quiet, comfortable and cool. Design your sleep environment to establish the conditions you need for sleep - cool, quiet, dark, comfortable and free of interruptions. Also make your bedroom reflective of the value you place on sleep. Check your room for noise or other distractions, including a bed partner's sleep disruptions such as snoring, light, and a dry or hot environment. Consider using blackout curtains, eye shades, ear plugs, humidifiers, fans and other devices.

Comfort Criteria: Sleep on a comfortable mattress and pillows. Make sure your mattress is comfortable and supportive. The one you have been using for years may have exceeded its life expectancy - about 9 or 10 years for most good quality mattresses. Have comfortable pillows and make the room attractive and inviting for sleep, but also free of allergens that might affect your sleep.

Bedrooms Are for Sleeping: Use your bedroom only for sleeping. It is best to take work materials, computers and televisions out of the sleeping environment. Use your bed only for sleep to strengthen the association between bed and sleep. If you associate a particular activity or item with anxiety about sleeping, omit it from your bedtime routine. For example, if looking at a bedroom clock makes you anxious about how much time you have before you must get up, move the clock out of sight.

Food Factors: Dining early is a good habit not just from the sleep point of view, but also for your digestive system. Finish eating at least 2–3 hours before your regular bedtime. Eating or drinking too much may make you less comfortable when settling down for bed. It is best to avoid a heavy meal too close to bedtime. Also, spicy foods may cause heartburn, which leads to difficulty in falling asleep and creates discomfort during the night. Try to restrict fluids close to bedtime to prevent the disturbance of going to the bathroom at night, though some people find milk or herbal, non-caffeinated teas to be soothing and a helpful part of a bedtime routine.

Great Foods: Food is an important part of destressing and relaxing. For a good sleep, try eating foods that are rich in vitamin B. In fact, Vitamin B3 is believed to be sleep-inducing. Eating whole grains, chicken, eggs, fish, nuts and especially apricots is considered beneficial. Magnesium- and calcium-rich foods like fish, nuts, dark green vegetables and seeds are also considered calming and sleep promoting. Bananas, figs, cottage cheese (paneer), eggs, milk and dates, which contain the sleep-inducing element called serotonin, are absolute must-eats if you want your forty winks.

Exercise: It is best to complete your workout at least a few hours before bedtime. In general, exercising regularly makes it easier to fall asleep and contributes to sounder sleep. However, exercising sporadically or right before going to bed will make falling asleep more difficult. In addition to making us more alert, our body temperature rises during exercise, and it takes as much as 6 hours to normalise. A cooler body temperature is useful in bringing on the sleep state. Finish your exercise at least 3 hours before bedtime. Late afternoon exercise is the perfect way to help you fall asleep at night.

Caffeine Problems: Avoid caffeine containing coffee, tea, soft drinks and chocolate close to bedtime. It can keep you awake. Caffeine is a stimulant, which means it can produce an alerting effect. Caffeine products, such as coffee, tea, colas and chocolate, remain in the body on average from 3 to 5 hours, but they can affect some people up to 12 hours later. Even if you do not think caffeine affects you, it may disrupt and alter your sleep quality. Avoiding caffeine within 6–8 hours of going to bed can help improve sleep quality.

Nicotine and Insomnia: Avoid nicotine-containing cigarettes, tobacco products. Used close to bedtime, such things can lead to poor sleep. Nicotine is also a stimulant; so smoking before bed makes it more difficult to fall asleep. When smokers go to sleep, they experience withdrawal symptoms from nicotine, which also cause sleep problems. Nicotine can cause difficulty in falling asleep, problems waking in the morning, and may also cause nightmares.

Alcohol Awakens: Avoid alcohol close to bed-time. Although many people think alcohols are sedatives, they actually disrupt sleep, causing night-time awakenings. Consuming alcohol leads to a night of less-restful sleep.

RECAP

- There is a strong relationship between the quantity and quality of one's sleep and many health problems.
- Insufficient sleep affects growth hormone secretion that is linked to obesity; as the amount of hormone secretion decreases, the chance for weight gain increases.
- Blood pressure usually falls during the sleep cycle. However, interrupted sleep can adversely affect this normal decline, leading to hypertension and cardiovascular problems.
- Insufficient sleep impairs the body's ability to use insulin, which can lead to the onset of diabetes.
- Deep and restorative sleep is essential for the body to recuperate and relax.
- Disturbed sleep does not help the body to unwind.
- Researchers have found that sleep is as essential to the body as nourishment.
- Research reveals that the brain derives the most refreshment and benefit from the big-wave levels of sleep that occur in the earlier cycles of the sleep period.

- The first hour or two of sleep goes immediately into the Delta wave level, which is relaxing and restorative.
- There is some truth in the saying that sleeping before midnight is better than sleeping in the early hours.

Using the Five Senses

Watching the movie *Black,* I realised how important our senses are. We take most of them for granted. But ask a person who is blind or deaf, and he will tell you how miserable it can be not to be able to see or hear the wonderful things that surround you. Yet, most of us do not utilise our senses to the fullest potential. We use the sense of hearing for just hearing, not as a de-stressing mechanism.

Although we have pursued various avenues for de-stressing ourselves, using the senses has been largely ignored. Yet, senses can be used very effectively to get rid of the anxiety and tension we suffer in our daily life.

Man is perhaps the only being in the animal kingdom that has such powerful and well-developed senses. Our five senses are like powerful antennae that cope with many challenges and provide many pleasures. The sense of touch enables us to enjoy the feel of velvet-smooth baby skin. The sense of smell allows us to differentiate between the sensuous whiff of musk or the mellow scent of rose. The sense of hearing helps us know the pleasure of soothing strains of melody. The sense of taste is the basic reason for a gourmet's existence.

Our palates are gifted with the taste buds that allow us the enjoyment of different kinds of food. The sense of sight allows us to see and appreciate the beauty around us. Can you imagine living without any of these sensory pleasures? The Chinese believe that our senses are united with the universe. Every molecule, every atom of the universe, is in constant vibration, vibrating on its own frequency and wavelength. The vibrations of sound, colour, smell, taste, heat and light enter our bodies constantly through all our senses.

When was the last time you paused long enough to really, I mean *really,* see and feel in your soul the beauty of a sunrise or the vibrancy of a sunset? How many of you turn off the noise of the world (including the radio, television, computer and other electronic things) to experience the benefits, in your mind and body, of the sounds of silence? When was the last time you ate a meal with enough mindfulness that you actually experienced and savoured the different flavours within each dish? When you received flowers, did you take time to really smell them – not only with your nose, but also with your heart?

For those of you who have all five of your senses: I hope you know how blessed you are. Recently, I ran into a childhood friend whom I had not seen for ages. As we caught up with the events in each other's life, she shared her sorrow with me.

'You know Tanu,' she said, 'I thought I had always appreciated my five senses, but it wasn't until I lost one of mine that I genuinely understood the value of each sense and treasure the four I have left.'

Three winters ago, she was hit hard by a virus that was going around at the time. After she recovered, she began to realise that she could no longer smell the ripened raspberry fragrance of her hand and body lotion.

'I couldn't smell the fresh scent of the lemon when I cut it for my salad. Then I realised I could not smell anything. Things began to taste strange. My favourite fruit, strawberries, tasted funny. After tests and medications, the doctor said there was nothing more he could do for me. I did some traditional Chinese medicine and now have my sense of taste back – but I have to rely on my memory for my olfactory sense. I never realised how much I relied on and used my sense of smell,' she ended with a wistful smile.

It is estimated that we take in 70 per cent of our sensory information through our sense of sight. I would venture a guess that most of us would say the sense of sight would be the hardest sense to lose.

When Helen Keller was asked, late in her life, what sensory loss she would deem the most debilitating, she immediately said, 'It is in sound that fundamental communication finds its essence, and human beings gain their greatest understanding of another's attitudes and feelings.'

Our lifestyle has become so rushed and hurried, so packed with long hours of work, emails, voicemails, meetings, family activities and commitments that we scarcely have the time to enjoy the blessedness of our senses to their optimum level. We are constantly being bombarded with multi-sensory stimuli, which eventually become overwhelming and stressful. We're moving though life with lightning speed, but not actually experiencing it. We're stressed, overwhelmed and fatigued. We need to rebalance ourselves and take time to pause and truly experience life through our senses in a calming, relaxing and rejuvenating way. When we connect with our senses mindfully, our senses can unite our mind, body and spirit. They can serve as a pathway to our innermost feelings and our inner wisdom. They can relax us, calm us and rejuvenate us.

So the next time you see a vibrant sunset, feel it with your body. Hear your next symphony with your soul. Savour the flavours of your next meal, not just with your tongue but with your nose and heart too. Touch a loved one's hand and feel the warmth of their touch in your heart. Smell your favourite fragrance with your whole being.

There are many, many different things you can do to stimulate your senses for relaxation and stress release. It would be a waste of God's precious gifts if we did not use the senses for optimum benefit. The senses can be a tremendous use and become a potent tool in relaxing our stressed minds and bodies. Most of the therapies stem out of the senses anyway. Whether it is massage, aromatherapy, music or visualisation – they are all linked to our senses.

1. Releasing Stress through the Sense of Sight

Almost 90 per cent of our sensory inputs come through the eyes. Deskbound people strain their eyes, and so do people who work on computers.Yet, this wonderful sense can be used superbly to function as a stress buster. Even eye specialists recommend staring at greenery for relaxing the eye. Mental relaxation can also be brought about through the sense of sight in a very effective manner.

Be on the lookout for a small pond, or small lake, in the early morning before the wind makes its mark on the water. Notice how still and calm the water is, so calm that you can see the trees, sky, clouds and all its surroundings reflected in the pond. (Naturalists refer to this as mirrored stillness.) Know that when you look at a still body of water, that image of peace and calm settles into your unconscious and promotes a deep sense of relaxation. Put that image of mirrored stillness in your memory bank and bring that image to your mind whenever you need to feel calm, peaceful and relaxed.

The sun that appears on the horizon each day to cheer us is taken for granted by most of us, till we find the constantly cloudy and sunless weather of the rainy season depressing us. We don't realise that the natural light from the sun raises our spirits and encourages health and well-being through the pineal gland. To know the value of sunlight, sit in a sun-bathed and warmed room on a winter morning and experience how great it feels. Light and colour create mood and atmosphere. Combined, they have the ability to dazzle or enhance, dim or brighten the mood.

Colour affects us emotionally, physically and spiritually and stimulates our senses by encouraging relaxation or activity. That is the reason why the green colour of nature can soothe tired eyes and the azure blue of the water waves can bring solace to the soul.

2. Releasing Stress through the Sense of Sound

When people talk of music for the soul, does it strike a

chord? There is music that energises you, music that relaxes you and music that calms your soul. Pleasing sounds encourage relaxation and are an important link with nature. Sound waves create vibrations in the ethereal layers around us, stimulating chi energy.

The most effective stress-releasing music is one that incorporates the natural sounds of birds, rustle of leaves, bubbling brooks, roar of sea waves, whales singing or falling rain. Pay attention to the healing sounds surrounding you, such as an indoor waterfall or a wind chime. Just being with nature and listening to the sounds of a stream or the chirping of birds can relax the mind and body. The primal energy of sound that comes from a simple chanting of Aum can bring about total relaxation and peace.

Music is very therapeutic, but silence is also important for physical and emotional health. Make an attempt to find some time to sit silently in a room and let your mind relax in silence. Silence has a very calming effect. Go through your CD collection and play the music that relaxes you and calms your soul. Make it a point to take time to listen to them every day. Listen to them when driving home from work, going for a walk, or when you get home after a long day at work. Think of it as music therapy for your mind, body and spirit.

3. Releasing Stress through the Sense of Smell

Scientists have learned that the part of the brain that registers olfactory sensations has neurons that store memory. That is why when you smell chocolate chip cookies baking it transports you back to you mother's or grandmother's kitchen. Our ability to remember what we've smelled is stronger than our ability to recall whatever we've seen. Thus, smells, memories and emotions are intrinsically linked. Think about places you like to go to when you want to relax. Then think about the scent or fragrances that are in the environment. Maybe it's the scent of a pine forest, the salty ocean air, orange blossoms or a campfire. Place herb pillows under your head at night or when you are taking a nap. This will bring a peaceful sleep and heal your mind while you slumber.

Just by placing bright and fragrant flowers all around the room, you can promote invigorating energy around you. Go to a candle shop and find an aromatic candle with the scent that reminds you of your favourite place. Then set aside time to burn the candle and let the fragrance take you to your peaceful place.

4. Releasing Stress through the Sense of Taste

In today's rushed lifestyle we 'wolf' down our food or eat on the run. Hurried eating robs the taste buds of pleasure. Imagine, a cook spends so much time to create a delicious dish, which takes just a few minutes for us to devour. This hurried gobbling of food creates more stress for the digestive system. Take time to actually taste and savour the flavours of the different foods you eat.

If you really want to clear your palate, wake up your taste buds and genuinely experience the sense of taste – chew on a fresh mint leaf for a few seconds. You could also help your taste buds by cleansing the palate between each course with plain bread or sips of water. It not only cleanses the palate but clears the mind as well. Close your eyes and focus your complete attention on the taste of mint. Then say 'ahh!' You may be pleasantly surprised how refreshed you feel. Perhaps it was to clear the taste buds that some of the ancient cultures required the bitter food to be eaten at first. Thereafter, everything else tasted like ambrosia.

5. Releasing Stress through the Sense of Touch

The sense of touch is so important that infants would die without it. Scientists have found that orphans, who are not touched and hugged, have a much slower rate of development than babies from happy families. The sense of touch is essential for life, not only through our fingers but every square inch of our bodies. Our skin is the largest organ of the body and needs to be fed. Muscle tension is the number-one symptom of stress. One of the best remedies is a full-body massage. If you have never had a professional massage, I think you are missing one of the finer experiences in life for stress release for the whole body–mind system. Certified massage therapists are trained to work the tension out of your muscles and bring you to a state of relaxed calm.

Every day we participate in life, yet there are many days that we let slip away without really experiencing the joys, wonders and sensations of life. Stress is a part of life. It's not whether we have stress in our life, it's how we react to it that makes the difference.

RECAP

- ❄ Our five senses are like powerful antennae that cope with many challenges and provide many pleasures.
- ❄ The Chinese believe that our senses are united with the universe. Every molecule, every atom of the universe, is in constant vibration, vibrating on its own frequency and wavelength. The vibrations of sound, colour, smell, taste, heat and light enter our bodies constantly through all our senses.
- ❄ It is estimated that we take in 70 per cent of our sensory information through our sense of sight.
- ❄ When we connect with our senses mindfully, our senses can serve as a pathway to our innermost feelings and our inner wisdom. They can relax us, calm us and rejuvenate us.
- ❄ When you look at a still body of water, that image of peace and calm settles into your unconscious and promotes a deep sense of relaxation.
- ❄ Pleasing sounds encourage relaxation and are an important link with nature. Sound waves create

vibrations in the ethereal layers around us, stimulating chi energy.

- Smells, memories and emotions are intrinsically linked. Just by placing bright and fragrant flowers all around the room, you can promote invigorating energy around you.

The Sense of Sight

Our eyes serve as the windows to the world. What we see and visualise finally results in the way we interpret things. The sense of sight can be used as a powerful tool for relaxing the body, mind and soul. Experts advise us to gaze at greenery when our eyes get tired. This is more important for people who work on computers or read for long hours. Greenery relaxes the eyes. The sense of sight can be used intelligently to de-stress.

One of the most effective therapies that involve the sense of sight is visualisation or imagery, as it is sometimes called. Visualisation is the process of focusing your concentration on an image of what you want and seeing it as already having fructified. It is a ritual of entering the inner recesses of your mind, and with the power of the subconscious mind, materialising the desired object, instance or circumstance.

In a way, visualisation is similar to daydreams and imaginations, but it brings a certain kind of discipline into them. Visualisation is not imagination, though the dividing line is very subtle. Imagination is an outward projection of the mind and has its foundation in desires and emotions.

When you imagine something, it is not necessarily backed by the power of the conscious will. The visual is weak, vague and somewhat distant, whereas visualisation is a picture created by the mind and involves the use of will power. Visualisation uses rules and laws of nature.

Visualisation is extensively taught and used today in all spheres of activity from the mental to the spiritual. As a source of power, it can be used to manifest much of what we may want or need. What you visualise is what you actualise. The brain is a great gift to us from the Creator. Made up of billions of cells that communicate and cooperate with each other to form sensory and motor areas, it also communicates with billions of brain cells throughout the body.

All inputs to the body through the nervous system, including sight, sounds, emotions, feelings, etc., are recorded in the brain right from prenatal days.

To practise visualisation, the mind's own creative powers may be stretched to the limit. There are no fixed rules, though one must always visualise only something positive and harmonious. You can create a mental image of a pleasant and relaxing place in your mind. Involve all your senses in the imagery – see the place, hear the sounds, smell the aromas, feel the temperature and the movement of the wind. Enjoy the location in your mind. Visualisation is the idea of visualising what you want to the point of it becoming reality. Visualising images requires more practice and experience. Start with very simple images such as a clear blue sky, and slowly progress to more complex images such as a meadow and surrounding woods.

Relaxation is a prerequisite to successful visualisation, just as calm and composed breathing is a precursor to successful relaxation.

Visualisation for Relaxation

One common use of visualisation in relaxation is to imagine a scene, place or event that you remember as peaceful, restful, beautiful and happy. You can bring all your senses into the image, with sounds of running water and birds, the smell of cut grass, the taste of cool and refreshing drink, the warmth of sun or the fragrance of fresh flowers. Use the imagined place as a retreat from places of stress and pressure.

Other uses of visualisation in relaxation involve mental pictures of stress flowing out of the body; or of stress, distractions and everyday concerns being folded away and locked into a padlocked chest. Use of visualisation is as flexible as the effort you put into developing images that meet your specific needs.

The Right Colour

Have you ever noticed that your mood dictates the kind of clothes and colours you choose to wear for the day? Some days you are in a vibrant mood and opt for the flashy colours, while on other days, your sombre mood makes you choose muted tones. Research has found that colours affect us in a very striking manner. They decide and control our moods in a very subtle way.

One fascinating relaxation therapy that is increasingly being explored by many people is colour therapy. Colours play a very important role in our lives although we remain blissfully unaware of their power over our minds and bodies. Ancient wisdom laid down a few guidelines for the lifestyle of people. Amongst those guidelines, factors like colours and sunlight played a very important role. Colour comes from daylight, which contains all eight colours of the spectrum: red, orange, yellow, green, turquoise, blue, violet and magenta. Our Vedas state that the human body is made of five elements - earth, water, fire, metal and air. Each of these has a complementary colour to create harmonious effect, e.g. earth is associated with the green colour, air with yellow, fire with red and water with blue.

There were particular colour codes, which were used for auspicious occasions, and each of them had a significant effect. Brides wore red because red is the colour of vitality and passion, it strengthens the life force, reflects will, strength and sexuality. Red stimulates the overall metabolism and deeper passions. It is used to remove fear, fatigue and anxiety. Widows wore white because white is the colour of purity and amplification. White contains the entire light spectrum, so it can purify the entire system. Similarly, black has been used as a colour of mourning in the West because black is a colour that reflects strength. It is the protective colour and has grounding and calming effect, especially on sensitive people.

Apart from using appropriate colours in clothing to affect moods, colour therapy is increasingly being used as a method of healing. It is used to treat mental, emotional and physical problems and is best used as a supportive therapy along with other natural methods of preserving health such as correct diet, adequate rest and relaxation, exercise, yogic asanas and so on.

Every substance on earth contains colour. Even the rays cast on earth by celestial bodies contain colour in the form of white light. The healing power of the sun has been recognised by man for thousands of years. To maintain good health, our bodies must be able to adequately absorb and use the right amount of sunlight. In colour therapy, the treatment of diseases is done by applying the correct colours for healing in a more concentrated form than sunlight. The rays of the sun contain seven different colours – violet, indigo, blue, green, yellow, orange and red. These are natural colours, which are highly beneficial to the maintenance of health and for healing diseases.

According to practitioners of colour therapy, the cause of any disease can be traced to the lack of a particular colour in the human system. Colour therapy is a technique of restoring imbalance by means of applying coloured light to the body. It was a popular method of cure even in ancient times. Some 2,500 years ago, Pythagoras applied coloured light for therapy and coloured halls were used for healing in ancient Egypt, China and India.

Colour and Perception

Colour is light which travels in waves. Each colour wavelength strikes the retina of the eye slightly differently and is converted into different electrical impulses accordingly. The colours observed by the eyes have a stimulating effect on the brain and the body. A colour has both negative and positive attributes. For example, magenta is the colour of 'letting go'. It can liberate you from destructive emotions, but too much of it can be mentally disturbing.

Recent neuropsychological studies have shown that around 80 per cent of all the information our senses receive about the world is of a visual nature and almost a third of grey cerebral matter is used to process this information. There is a specific area inside the brain in which information is encoded expressly according to colour, regardless of the visual form of the perceived object.

Our everyday experience proves that colour influences our state of mind and our feelings. Many disciplines such us architecture, town planning, ergonomics, medicine - including psychology - have begun to pay more and more attention to the effects of colour on the human psyche and body.

Hospital walls are often painted blue because of its soothing effect on patients who are often suffering from emotional stress. The surgeons' robes are green - the opposite colour to red - in order to nullify the images provoked by looking for long periods of time at the red of blood and body tissues.

Some shades of yellow provoke a sense of nausea and therefore are never used in airplanes. Blue light has been found to lower blood pressure by calming the autonomic nervous system, while red light causes it to rise. Bright red on walls causes uneasiness in the occupants of a room. In one instance, the designers of a large factory of Japanese cars painted the walls of the toilets in red colour to reduce the time employees spent loitering inside it.

Research has also shown that colour-tinted eyeglasses can be highly effective in the treatment of learning difficulties, notably dyslexia. This was first discovered by psychologist Helen Irlen, but was regarded sceptically until recent investigations by the British Medical Research Council confirmed Irlen's claims.

This was amply proved by the reports of the governor of a newly-built prison in which each of its four wings had been painted a different colour. Both he and his staff found that the behaviour of the prisoners varied significantly depending on which wing they lived in, although their allocation to each had been random. Those in red and yellow wings were more inclined to violence than those in the blue and green wings.

Experimental research lends support to these observations. Viewing red light has been found to increase the subjects' strength by 13.5 per cent and to elicit 5.8 per cent more electrical activity in the arm muscles. For this reason it is now used to improve the performance of athletes. Whereas red light appears to help athletes who need short, quick bursts of energy, blue light assists in performances requiring a more steady energy output.

By comparison, pink has been found to have a tranquillising and calming effect within minutes of exposure. It suppresses hostile, aggressive and anxious behaviour - could that be the reason of its traditional association with women in western culture? Pink-coloured prison cells are now widely used to reduce violent and aggressive behaviour among prisoners in the West, and some sources have reported a reduction of muscle strength in inmates within 2.7 seconds. It appears that when in pink surroundings, people cannot be aggressive even if they want to, because the colour saps their energy.

The endocrine glands are also associated with certain specific colours for their optimum functioning. The brain releases norephinephrine, a chemical that inhibits the specific hormones that contribute to aggressive behaviour when exposed to certain colours. For instance, red vibrations increase blood pressure and increase respiratory functions due to the pituitary gland coming into play. It takes a fraction of a second for the gland to send a signal for the release of adrenaline. This causes physiological and metabolic changes.

Yellow colour significantly adds to stress and a flare-up of allergies. Blue produces a calming effect by triggering the secretion of no less than eleven neurotransmitters that bring a tranquillising effect on the people exposed to this colour. Green colour enhances the production of histamine in the blood, increasing immunity against allergic reactions, relaxing eye muscles, alleviating high level of stress besides soothing the body cells.

The colour brown is also helpful in balancing the homeostatic levels of the body. This helps in reducing tension, erasing fatigue, and diminishing irritability and impatience. Brown stimulates the release of prostaglandin, which harmonises many bodily functions, improving them substantially. The level of tryptophan amino acids is also increased by exposure to this colour. Tryptophan amino acids influence sleep, moods and immunity levels.

A Powerful Relaxation Technique

Combining Visualisation with colour therapy can be one of the most powerful techniques in relaxing both the mind and the soul. I devised this technique along with that of Reiki for myself in times of extreme distress and found it to work exceptionally well. This technique can be used to heal the mind through colour-cleansing of the chakras.

A Word about Chakras and Aura

The chakras are the seven main energy centres of the body, and aura is our energy field, which some gifted individuals claim to see as a haze of coloured light surrounding the body. The colours in the aura have their own significance and are affected by our health and energy quality. It has been found that the aura of bodies, when exposed to colour therapy, alter their effect dramatically. They trigger a series of changes in the systems, organs and cells. Before you discard the importance of aura and chakras, let me tell you that scientific research and Kirlian photography have proved the existence of these elements in the body.

The six nerve centres, seven major chakras and many subsidiary chakras can be influenced through chromotherapy. The chakras are stations along the central axis of your being. Each one is a point at which energy can be expressed in a certain set of actions, attitudes and emotions. The chakras are a map of the soul, which you must move along for healing to happen. These points represent our physical, mental, emotional and spiritual growth. When these points are healthy and in balance, we remain in peak health.

The chakras are bell-shaped vortices, which are the whirling centres of power. Each of them is associated with a specific colour and these colours have a healing effect and energising effect on the chakra and the organs controlled by them. Each of the chakras spins at a varying rate producing far-reaching effects on the body.

The combined power of the chakras, colour and visualisation can work in an amazing manner to bring comfort and a tranquillising effect on the brain. This is how you do it:

- Select a quiet room that is cool and comfortable. A little bit of darkened effect quickens the ability to relax so pull the drapes over your windows.
- Switch off your mobile and unhook the telephone. In short, there should be no disturbance or interruption, whatsoever.
- Lie flat on your back and close your eyes. The exercise should preferably be performed on the floor. Use a carpet or a mat to lie on.
- Let the body muscles relax slowly, starting from the toes to the head. Become aware of each muscle and loosen it wilfully. Continue this exercise till you begin to feel totally relaxed.
- At first it may seem difficult. but with a little practice you will find that the body goes into relaxed mode almost immediately.
- Now concentrate on your breath. Sense your breath moving in and out of your nostrils.

- At you concentrate, you will be able to feel the warmth of the exhaled air and the coolness of the inhaled air.
- At this stage you should be able to hear your heartbeats and feel the pumping action of your heart.
- Visualise yourself at the beach with the rolling of blue waves around you. You are lying on the golden sands with palm fronds waving above you. All around you is a beautiful forest of green trees. Waves from the sea are touching your toes and you can feel the cool breeze fanning your body. Just as with meditation, at first visualisation seems a bit difficult, but if you let your mind relax, it comes easily. Let go of your anxious thoughts replacing them with visual pictures in the mind.
- As the scenery becomes almost real, focus on your heart chakra and feel it spinning with great energy. Visualise it being surrounded by a giant, green, glowing orb, washing the chakra lovingly.
- As you visualise the chakra being tended by the loving hands of the green colour, you will feel peace descending on your mind. There will be a cool aura around you.
- Shift your focus to the throat chakra. A lump will rise at that part of your body as you shift your attention to it. Visualise a blue satin material enveloping the throat in a loving manner, wiping away all impurities from it. It is awash with a soft blue light, purifying and soothing.
- As the throat is washed clean of all stress and worries, focus your attention on the Ajna chakra, which lies between your brows. This is the seat of your third eye. A powerful energy emanates from this region. The Ajna chakra energy has much to do with the emotional intelligence and clears all kinds of emotional confusion.

- The third eye is influenced by the colour indigo. So envelop the seat of this chakra with this colour to bring tranquillity and peace to your soul. Imagine the indigo flame with its cool and luminescent light radiating all around the Ajna chakra.
- As the third eye is cleansed of all stress, move down up to the crown chakra. This is the most powerful chakra associated with spirituality, divinity and super consciousness. It guides the mind into the path of wisdom, bliss and spiritual power. The colour violet is associated with crown chakra, and this is the colour that you must visualise as you focus your attention on the sahasrara chakra. See the soothing, soft petals of violet flower caressing your crown, bringing a sensation of comfort, calm and placid contentment to your being.
- Lastly, let the feelings of calmness flow through you as you inhale deeply. With practice you will literally feel the elevation of your soul.

When done properly, this exercise will rejuvenate and refresh your entire body, mind and soul. It should recharge your energy and dispel all stress and fatigue.

Recap

- The sense of sight can be used as a powerful tool for relaxing the body, mind and soul.
- One of the most effective therapies that involve the sense of sight is visualisation. Visualisation is the process of focusing your concentration on an image of what you want and seeing it as already having fructified.
- Colour therapy is increasingly being used as a method of promoting relaxation. It is used to treat mental, emotional and physical problems

and is best used as a supportive therapy along with other natural methods of preserving health such as correct diet, adequate rest and relaxation, exercise, yogic asanas, etc.

- Combining visualisation with colour therapy can be one of the most powerful techniques in relaxing both the mind and the soul.

THE SENSE OF HEARING

Contemplate for a Moment: Why do we feel relaxed where the sea or the palm trees surround us. The soft swish of the leaves, the lapping sound of waves and the chirping of birds are sounds that soothe and de-stress us. At the same time, the loud noise created by cacophonous music, traffic, industrial noise or the sound of hammering, can get us stressed.

Research has proved that those who reside near railway stations or airports or bus terminus are more prone to stress-related health problems, while those who stay in rural areas, close to nature and enjoy the natural rhythms of life, are least prone to stress.

We talk of our hearts singing with joy when we are happy. We sing whenever we are happy and full of pleasure.

Life has a rhythmic pattern just as music. According to occult experts, every human being is made up of a tremendous number of vibrations. Music too is based on vibrations. We begin a project with the burst of energy, carry it to the climax, and then we are spent, so we need to rest. In the melodic rhythm of life there is always the beginning followed up by the build-up, then the climax that leads to the release of tension and finally the rest. If we break the pattern, we suffer.

What makes sound have such immense effect on our stress levels?

Like every other sense, our sense of hearing has a huge effect on our body and mind. It can generate stress-producing hormones or reduce them according to the kind of sounds that surround us.

Recent studies have revealed a new therapy known as music therapy and the experts claim that it has an enormous potential in healing both the body and the mind. Psychologists have already discovered the effect soft and soothing music has on the minds of the people who have lost sanity. Even babies have been known to respond favourably to soothing music. The effect of pleasing sound has been noticed more on the disturbed minds, which are excessively stressed.

How could human beings remain impervious to pleasant sound when animals and plants are known to be affected by music?

Lately, music therapy has been used quite successfully in stress release, inducing sleep, relaxation and other psychosomatic problems. Besides bringing a relaxed state to the body and mind, music also has a soul-elevating effect. Scientific studies have evaluated the merits of music therapy. Research indicates that certain forms of music can produce physiological as well as psychological benefits. The result is increased wellness and quality of life regardless of one's health.

Certain kinds of music stimulate the lower and base senses. The fast and throbbing beats of the disco, pop and other kind of remix music that is popular these days disturb the mind and agitate the senses. They appeal to our physical self and create high energy, which could sometimes lead to aggressive behaviour. It is generally classical music that is particularly appealing to the higher senses and elevates the mind to a spiritual level.

Music that stimulates anger and sexual emotions is more harmful than good. This music controls and disturbs us. It manipulates us into feeling things that don't help us.

Most types of music have an effect on our body or on our emotions. Some kinds of music bring our mind to a higher, subtler state in which we sense inner peace. Most classical western music (like Mozart's and Beethoven's) affects our emotions and to a small extent, our body. The right kind of music can help in the treatment of anxiety, depression, terminal illness, pain management and facilitate the grieving process.

Music therapists work with all patient groups such as the terminally-ill, premature infants, chronic pain sufferers, the physically and mentally disabled, Alzheimer's patients and victims of other forms of dementia. Practitioners confirm that the healing powers of music helps terminally-ill patients decrease their anxiety, depression and pain. Music also reduces the agitation that often accompanies Alzheimer's disease.

(National Association for Music Therapy)

Music exalts each Joy,
Allays each Grief,
Expels Diseases,
Softens every Pain,
Subdues the rage of
Poison and the Plague.

From *The Art of Preserving Health,*
Book IV, By John Armstrong

Mantra Chanting

Chanting quietens the mind! It has the power to cleanse the soul and energise the thoughts, drive out the negative and usher in the positive vibrations. Devotional chanting can take your negative energy and turn it into positive energy.

Chanting of mantras produces powerful cosmic vibrations that fill up the atmosphere like a golden mist, and the positive power pervades our beings with beneficial effects. When we chant, we forget all our worries and concentrate on the words of the mantra. This causes ebb and flow of stress in our bodies and minds.

In the course of his job, my husband has to travel quite frequently. During these trips he is highly stressed, as the deadlines have to be maintained. On one such trip, he was staying in a Circuit House with Subhash Joshi, another officer. Early in the morning, he heard Joshi chanting mantras loudly as he walked about the corridor. Surprised, my husband asked him why he was chanting. 'It clears my mind and makes me peaceful. The best part is that I remain in a good mood through out the day,' Joshi replied.

After the breakfast my husband was pacing the corridor in great agitation. He was getting late for his meeting and the driver of the hired car hadn't turned up. He shouted angrily at the driver the moment the car arrived. Minutes later, they were off for the meeting. Joshi smiled at my scowling husband and said: 'This, sir, is the difference. I did not get worked up or angry because of my mental peace.'

After that incident, chanting has become a regular habit with my husband.

There is no doubt that beginning the morning with religious prayers, chants or spiritual music makes the spirit calm and the mind peaceful. You are able to handle the day's stress in a more efficient manner.

Of all the mantras that are popular across the world, Aum occupies a prime place.

The goal which all the Vedas declare, which all austerities aim at, and which men desire when they lead the life of continence ... is Aum. This syllable Aum is indeed Brahman. Whosoever knows this syllable obtains all that he desires. This is the best support; this is the highest support. Whosoever knows this support is adored in the world of Brahma.

—Katha Upanishad

Aum changed its form as it travelled round the world. In Tibet, it became the sacred word hum, in the Islamic countries it transformed into amin, and for the Egyptians, Greeks, Romans and Christians it became amen. In Hebrew, amen means 'sure, faithful'.

Aum is not a word but rather an intonation, which, like music, transcends the barriers of age, race, culture and even species. It is made up of three Sanskrit letters, aa, au and mm which, when combined together, make the sound Aum or Om. It is believed to be the basic sound of the universe and to contain all other sounds. It is a prayer in itself. If repeated with the correct intonation, it can resonate throughout the body so that the sound penetrates to the centre of one's being, the atman or the soul.

Swami Yogananda noted that everything in the universe is composed of energy and that the apparent differentiation between solids, liquids, gases, sound and light is merely a difference in their vibratory rates. He maintained that by chanting Aum, the divine vibration, we can increase the body's supply of cosmic energy and even direct it as a healing force to any part of the body, mind and soul.

It is said that 12,000 recitations of Aum remove all sins, while 12,000 recitations daily for a period of one year bring realisation of the Absolute (brahman). If that seems a little overwhelming, simple try chanting Aum in your daily meditation and let the incredible power of sound and vibration work for you. Aum will bring your mind to focus.

Paramahansa Yogananda called it 'the vibration of the Cosmic Motor'. The great father of yoga, Patanjali, advised using it to overcome the obstacles and distractions in life. 'Audible utterance of Aum produces a sense of sacredness.'

Aum is a way of deepening the concentration of the mind, which leads to realisation of the divine. As you chant it, surrender to the vibrations of Aum. Feel your awareness expanding into the field of pure consciousness.

'The letter A symbolises the conscious or waking state,' according to the yoga expert, BKS Iyengar. 'The letter U the dream state, and the letter M the dreamless sleep state of the mind and spirit.' The entire symbol, Iyengar says, stands for the 'realisation of man's divinity within himself'.

The simple syllables are omnipotent and immensely healing, especially if chanted during meditation. While meditating, when we chant Aum, we create within ourselves a vibration that attunes with the cosmic vibration.

Recap

- The sense of hearing can be used effectively to relax the body and mind. We talk of our hearts singing with joy when we are happy. We sing whenever we are happy and full of pleasure.
- Like every other sense, our sense of hearing has a huge effect on our body and mind. It can generate stress-producing hormones or reduce them, according to the kind of sounds that surround us.
- Music therapy has been used quite successfully in stress release, inducing sleep, relaxation and other psychosomatic problems.
- Chanting quietens the mind! It has the power to cleanse the soul and energise the thoughts, drive out the negative and usher in the positive vibrations.

The Sense of Smell

Our sense of smell has a very important role to play in relaxation of the body, mind and soul. Have you ever noticed how you associate different smells with the events of your life? Some odours invoke nostalgic memories of happy times while others bring morbid thoughts to your mind. Most people love the smell of earth after the first shower of rain. It relaxes the mind and makes the mood light. You remember some people by the perfumes they use. The fragrance of a flower can immediately lead you to the happy days of your childhood.

Research has found that identifying ten kinds of odours can help the detection of dementia. Those who went on to develop Alzheimer's disease performed poorly in terms of identifying the smell of lemon, lilac, leather, clove, menthol, pineapple, strawberry, natural gas, soap and smoke. According to a recent study held by the America College of Neuro-psycho-pharmacology, the sense of smell is one of the first things that go when someone develops dementia.

We can use the sense of smell efficiently to create holistic relaxation. That is what makes aromatherapy so important.

Aromatherapy for Relaxation

One of the most primitive forms of medicine involved burning aromatic plants in order to 'smoke' illness out of a patient. This process was frequently linked with various rituals and religious practices, and sometimes plants with soothing properties were burnt too, to create a mystical and spiritual experience as part of the healing ritual. The use of incense in the ceremonies of diverse religions through the centuries has perpetuated this aspect; many of the gums and resins that are used in incense have powerful therapeutic properties - for example, as respiratory antiseptics - as well as induce a meditative, reflective state of mind in the worshippers.

Aromatic plants and extracts have been highly regarded by all the greater ancient civilisations stretching through the Middle East from Babylonia and Persia to India and China. The oldest medical texts from these countries, dating back at least 3000 years, list many aromatic plants and their uses. Some of the most detailed descriptions are to be found in ancient Egyptian writings; fragrant plants were employed in all aspects of life, from perfume and cosmetics to medicine and in the rituals for embalming the dead.

Some of the ointment jars excavated from Tutankhamen's tomb contained preservative resins such as frankincense, which still had an odour after some 3200 years. Hieroglyphics from as far back as 4500 BC confirm that the ancient Egyptians used aromatic substances in medicine.

The Egyptians were acutely aware of the value of fragrance in enhancing mood and developed a reputation as masters of perfumery. Cleopatra may have owed something of her fabled attractiveness to Julius Caesar and Mark Antony from her use of vast amounts of rose petals to scent her living quarters. Cleopatra and Nurjahan must have been soul sisters, for Nurjahan too used roses liberally. Jahangir, like Julius Caesar, was enamoured by his empress.

Interestingly, however, the Egyptians do not appear to have discovered the process of distilling the essential oils from plants, relying instead on infused oils and ointments. These were later widely used by the Greeks and Romans, both as medicine and as part of the daily ritual of public bathing, which the Romans, in particular, so enjoyed.

The Roman armies employed many Greek physicians, who carried the knowledge of aromatic and other plants across many countries. Galen, who rose to be the personal physician to the emperor Marcus Aurelius, invented the original cold cream and was a great writer on all matters concerning health and medicines. His and other works formed the basis of medicine for many centuries, and with the decline of the Roman Empire, much of this knowledge went eastwards into Byzantium. It was the Arabic countries that made the next great leap forward in aromatherapy. By the ninth century, Baghdad was thriving partly due to being the centre of the rose industry, exporting rose water as far as India. The principle of distillation was first applied to roses and is generally credited to Abu Ali Ibn Sina, better known as Avicenna (980–1037), a philosopher and physician from Uzbekistan. Steam distillation enabled the pure essential oil to be extracted from many plants.

In the West, aromatic infused oils had continued to be used, and during the period of the crusades, essential oils, or 'perfumes of Arabia' as they were known, spread extensively throughout Europe. As the gums and resins of Asia were not easily available, native Mediterranean plants such as rosemary and lavender were used for making essential oils too. The French were particularly enthusiastic in adopting these oils, laying the foundations for today's perfumery industry as well as therapeutic uses.

Burning antiseptic herbs such as thyme and rosemary to fumigate the air and ward off disease was carried out in several French hospitals until well into the 20th century. It was a Frenchman, Rene Gattefosse, a chemist working in the perfumery industry, who coined the term aromatherapy some 50 years ago. He burnt his hand badly in an accident in his laboratory. He used essential oil of lavender to cool the tissue and found it healed the burnt flesh remarkably quickly, with no infection or scar. During both World Wars, essential oils were used to treat wounds and infections, and one of the pioneers of this work was Dr Jean Valnet, who published his findings in the late 1960s. Respected medical establishments in France are now looking at the medicinal aspects of essential oils.

Modern research has confirmed the therapeutic properties of essential oils. At Milan University, for example, depression and anxiety have been successfully treated by Dr Paolo Rovesti, using aerosol sprayed oils, and in the USSR, a type of eucalyptus oil has been found beneficial in the treatment of a strain of influenza – an important finding, since very few natural anti-viral agents have been identified.

The power of aromatic plants extends beyond antiseptic or anti-inflammatory properties. It is well established that scent can evoke memories, change people's moods and make them feel good. Aromatherapy has developed in the UK the US and many other countries in the last 20 years into a holistic system that tries to heal and balance the whole person. The oils are often incorporated into massage or used in baths or simply evaporated into the air in a burner to improve physical and emotional well-being.

A useful guideline when using essential oils at home – for instance, the bath – is the 1–2 rule. Use only one or two oils together at any time; use 1 or 2 drops in the bath, and do not use any particular oil on a daily basis for more than 1 or at most 2 weeks.

Some essential oils have a stimulating effect on the uterine muscles and should therefore not be used if you are pregnant, or suspect you might be. The possibly problematic oils to be avoided during your pregnancy include basil, clary sage, fennel, hyssop, juniper, pennyroyal, peppermint, sage and thyme. Equally, if you ever get any skin irritation or allergic reaction to any oil, then you should of course stop using it.

Oils in the Air

A widely-used method for relaxation is to use essential oils to spread aroma in the rooms by means of a vaporiser or oil burner. Vaporisers are widely available and range from the simple utilitarian version to the highly decorative, hand-crafted piece. Although they come in many forms, they all work on the same principle. The reservoir, or receptacle, is filled with water, to which drops of essential oils are added. The reservoir is then heated, causing the water to evaporate and the warm oil to release its perfume.

The simplest type of vaporiser makes use of a candle as the heat source; a more efficient but more expensive type is the electric vaporiser. Under certain circumstances, these are preferable to the type heated by a candle – for example in the reception area of an office, in a hospital ward or at home, when you want to disperse oils for a long period of time without the necessity of frequent supervision. Some electric vaporisers have a silent fan that disperses the evaporating oils; others employ a heated ceramic dish. Either would be suitable for a child's bedroom or a room occupied by someone who is bedridden. Whenever you use a vaporiser of any kind, do make certain that you place the burner in a safe position out of the reach of children and pets.

The number of drops of oil used in a burner depends on the size of the room: 2–3 drops for a small room, and as many as 6–10 drops for a larger one. It is better to use fewer drops and refresh the burner more frequently rather than use too many and saturate a room with scent.

If you do not have a vaporiser, or you feel the need for an instant aromatherapy treatment, try applying just a few drops of oil to a handkerchief or paper towel and gently inhaling the perfume. Placing the handkerchief on your pillow at night should ease breathing if you have a blocked nose; some oils will help promote a good night's sleep. It is not wise to take essential oils as a medicine except on the advice of a practitioner, but some people do use essential oils in tea, adding two or three drops of a suitable oil to a pot of black tea for digestive problems, urinary problems or stress.

Oils in Water

One of the most pleasant ways of using aromatic oils is to put 1–2 drops into a bath just before you get in; they form a thin film over the surface of the water, which coats and penetrates the skin while you lie in the heady aroma. If you have a very dry skin, try adding a couple of drops of chosen essential oil to a teaspoonful of pure vegetable oil, such as sweet almond, and pour this into the bath.

On the emotional level, several essences have quite remarkable effects in helping to keep our moods in balance. The best anti-depressant oil is undoubtedly bergamot, and this can be used to ward off low vitality at times of stress and depression. A note of caution though - bergamot increases sensitivity to the sun, so prevent the overuse of this essence before exposure to bright sunlight.

Other mood elevators are neroli (or orange blossom), jasmine, melissa and rose.

Oils in Massage

For direct use on the skin, essential oils must be diluted. Use a good, pure vegetable oil as the base, such as coconut, apricot kernel, jojoba (actually a liquid wax) or sweet almond. If your skin tends to be very dry, add about 10 per cent of avocado or wheatgerm oil to the blend - avoid the latter if you are allergic to wheat. The essential oils are added at 1–2 per cent; assuming 20 drops to 1 ml, this means using 1 or 2 drops per 5 ml (1tsp) of base oil.

All the above suggestions for bath oils apply equally to aromatherapy message.

The healing properties of different aromatherapy oils

Aromatherapy Oil	**Properties and Benefits**
Lavender	Antiseptic, anti-depressant, healing; relieves stress and insomnia, soothes insect bites.
Rose	Anti-depressant, aphrodisiac, tonic; helpful for menstrual disorders; aids sleep.
Bergamot	Antiseptic, astringent, stimulative; helps to combat oily skin but can sensitise it to UV light.
Sandalwood	Healing, antiseptic; can relieve fluid retention, cystitis and insomnia.
Patchouli	Healing, soothing; helps combat dandruff and dry skin patches.
Ylang -Ylang	Antiseptic, aphrodisiac, tonic.
Myrrh	Healing, antiseptic, claming; eases viral and fungal infections such as thrush (if added to a bath).
Juniper	Diuretic, antiseptic, cleansing, calming; avoid in first five months of pregnancy, not to be used by those with kidney disease.
Neroli	Calming; soothes nerves and upset stomachs; a good remedy for dry skin.
Chamomile, Roman	The most soothing oil; relieves anxiety, stress, allergies, and pre-menstrual syndrome (PMS).
Basil	Reviving, decongestive.

Rosemary	Antiseptic, stimulating, balancing, diuretic, uplifting; not to be used in the first five months of pregnancy, or those with high blood pressure.
Frankincense	Decongestive, relaxing; aids sleep.

An Effective Relaxation Therapy

- Add a few drops of lavender, neroli or frankin cense in your bath water.
- Step in and soak for ten minutes.
- While the body is soaking in the goodness of the essence, switch your mind into the meditative mode.
- Take three deep breaths and close your eyes.
- Relax your mind and breathe in fully.
- With each breath, repeat the affirmation – 'I am totally relaxed. All the stress has drained out of my body. I feel rejuvenated and energised.'
- Be aware of your breath.
- Step out of your bath and feel the difference.
- You can also try flower remedies such as Bach White chestnut or Rock Rose to help you relax.
- The essential aromatherapy oils ylang-ylang, valerian, camomile and lavender applied in firm stroking movements to your forehead and chest will calm you down.

RECAP

- Our sense of smell has a very important role to play in relaxation of the body, mind and soul.
- We can use the sense of smell efficiently to create holistic relaxation. That is what makes aromatherapy so important.

- ❄ Essential oils can be used in various ways to bring relaxation. They can be used in vaporisers, in oil or water. Aromatic candles are a great way to spread the fragrance in the room. Essential oils, when used in baths or for massage, bring quick relaxation.

The Sense of Taste

It is a common knowledge that people use food as soothers during extreme stress and depressive phases. Stressed and lonely people are known to eat much more than the relaxed ones. Food of the right kind has been found to have an immensely healing effect on our bodies as well as minds. When we talk about food as a calming agent, we actually refer to the soothing effect it has on our taste buds, which transmit the comforting experience to the neurons in the brain.

A calm mind is one that is not disturbed by tension or anxiety. Such a mind should be able to work peacefully in any environment and face any challenge that life brings with it without getting upset. It would be able to look beyond the mundane affairs and be able to live with equanimity and balance. One would argue that prayers, meditation and a philosophical attitude should help attain that goal. No doubt about that, none at all. But life is not so simple. Sometimes, despite all the things we read and the strictures we follow, our mind becomes restless. Wrong food can also lead to an agitated mind. Just as scientists have discovered that food can control mood, make us think sharp, lead the brain to work better, they also found that certain kinds of food could have an adverse effect on the mind.

Calming Food

It has been found that eating carbohydrates without protein has a calming effect. How calming depends on the type of carbohydrates and the amount and time of day they are eaten. Eating carbohydrates that are low on the Glycemic Index will promote the more focused and calming aspect of serotonin release and less of the sleepy, sluggish feeling that is generally felt after eating heavy carbohydrate containing foods.

Brown rice, buckwheat, whole-grain rye bread, sourdough rye bread, pita bread, sweet potato, most wheat pastas are all Low-Glycemic Carbohydrates.

Complex carbohydrates increase levels of serotonin, the brain chemical known for its calming properties. Adequate levels of serotonin promote feelings of serenity, security and tranquillity. If you are too stressed out at the end of the day and need to wind down, it might help to eat brown rice, pasta, noodles, couscous and potato dishes with your evening meals. For a calming effect you could try some of the more interesting pasta types such as corn, rice and legume. Anxiety, fretfulness, an overactive mind, irritability and sleeplessness can be eased by eating foods that contain complex carbohydrates. A small bowl of muesli or oat-based cereal or a mashed banana (try it with a teaspoon of cold pressed honey drizzled over), about an hour before bed, might help encourage a sound sleep.

Researchers have found that the serotonin levels drop pre-menstrually, which may explain why women often feel more stressed, irritable, clumsy or depressed just before a period. It is due to this drop in the serotonin that they suffer cravings for sweet and starchy foods.

A new food concept has hit the stressed people in the recent times. Known as comfort food, these are the carbo-high food items that create a sense of wellness and combat stress. Some people consider oats, usually associated with breakfast foods as comfort food – another reason why an oat-based cereal could make a soothing snack.

Whole grains such as oats, brown rice, rye, millet, barley and couscous are excellent suppliers of B group vitamins. Lettuce contains beta-carotene, potassium, vitamin C and some calcium. Herbalists often use it as a calming food. Yoghurt and other forms of milk contain tryptophan, which the brain converts into the soothing chemical, serotonin. The complex carbohydrates found in brown rice may increase the level of serotonin, known for its calming properties. High carbohydrate root vegetables can help boost serotonin, the stress-busting and tranquillising hormone. Ginger is known to be calming to a stressed or upset digestive system.

You may have jokingly referred to yourself as a chocoholic or a sugarholic because of your sweet tooth, but researchers in New Jersey have found that sugar can have an effect on the body similar to addictive drugs. Sugar and sweets appeared to cause the brain to produce the same kind of pleasure-causing chemicals that drugs produce.

Food can relieve anxiety and bring a feel-good effect. Certain foods can act as tranquillisers and help you retain your equanimity.

During stress, the body needs more of certain nutrients because they are burned up faster than usual. Stress increases the demand for vitamin C, vitamin A, vitamin B-complex, proteins, magnesium, antioxidants and essential oils. To counteract the stress effects, one needs more of these nutrients.

There is a high concentration of vitamin C in our brain tissues, more than any other tissue in the body. Vitamin C is a powerful antioxidant, which is used up quickly during the stressful periods. One needs to cater to the high demand for this vitamin during the high levels of stress. An amount between 500–1,000 milligrams would be required to combat the stress after effects. The best sources of vitamin C are citrus fruits like oranges, potatoes, tomatoes and leafy green vegetables.

Vitamin A is another requirement during times of stress. It is needed for maintenance of skin, mucous membranes, bones, teeth and hair, eyesight and reproduction. Vitamin A may also protect against cancer. Liver (especially fish liver), egg yolk, fortified margarine, oily fish, oranges, apricots, carrots, tomatoes, melons and dark green leafy vegetables contain this vitamin in abundance.

Magnesium is found in dark green leafy vegetables, nuts, seeds, whole grain foods, legumes and milk.

Stress increases the generation of free radicals in the body. These free radicals damage the body cells and are the main cause of cancer. The only elements that can fight free radicals are antioxidants. Antioxidants are found in plenty in cruciferous vegetables like cabbage, cauliflower, broccoli, etc. They are rich in bio-flavinoids, which are powerful antioxidants.

Another important source of antioxidants is green tea. It contains an abundance of polyphenols, which are active agents protecting against heart disease and cancer. The polyphenols also protect against the damages caused by stress. Chamomile tea is a powerful anti-stress agent. It relaxes and soothes the mind and promotes sound sleep.

Fruits could provide the required amounts of antioxidants required to counteract stress. They contain simple sugars and complex carbohydrates, which help raise the serotonin levels in the bloodstream. Serotonins are the 'feel good' neurotransmitters, which elevate mood and fight depression.

Vegetable and fruit juices are also a good source of antioxidants. A regular glass of any fruit juice or vegetable juice can go a long way in helping the body to cope with the detrimental effects of stress.

Recap

- Food has been found to have an immensely healing effect on our bodies as well as minds.
- Scientists have discovered that food can control mood, make us think sharp, lead the brain to work better. They have also found that food could have a calming effect on the mind.
- Complex carbohydrates increase levels of serotonin, the brain chemical known for its calming properties.

- Serotonins are the 'feel good' neurotransmitters, which elevate mood and fight depression.
- If you are too stressed out at the end of the day and need to wind down, it might help to eat brown rice, pasta, noodles, couscous and potato dishes with your evening meals.
- For a calming effect you could try some of the more interesting pasta types such as corn, rice and legume.
- Eating foods that contain complex carbohydrates can ease anxiety, fretfulness, an overactive mind, irritability and sleeplessness.
- A small bowl of muesli or oat-based cereal, or a mashed banana (try it with a teaspoon of cold pressed honey drizzled over), about an hour before bed, might help encourage sound sleep.

The Sense of Touch

Why do we hug people or pat their shoulders to show our approval? Why do we hug them to share their grief? And why do you hold someone's hand during the period of trial?

These little gestures convey more sympathy and love than all the words put together. Touching is the more primitive way of expressing your feelings. Whether you hit out to express your anger or shake hands to express friendliness, every kind of human contact is an expression of our feelings.

We need the sense of touch to soothe and calm us during stressful times. More and more studies are confirming that just being touched regularly can boost mental and physical powers and improve quality of life for just about everyone – sick and well, young and old alike. We now know that human beings who don't get touched enough simply don't thrive, physically or emotionally.

Less well-known – but increasingly documented even by mainstream researchers – are all the ways a little 'hands-on' can help speed healing, improve thinking skills and even help relieve pain and other chronic ailments. Continued research is revealing that regular massage can even improve your overall health, mental faculties and create a feeling of wellness.

Our skin is perhaps the most sensitive of all sense organs. The biggest sensory organ in our body is the skin. It stretches all over our body and provides a tremendous range of uses to us. Sex therapists have been advocating the use of touch treatment to bring intimacy between couples.

The sense of touch can be used with tremendous possibilities, for relaxation. What better therapy can there be than the massage therapy, to induce a feeling of relaxation?

Massage for Relaxation

It's no secret that a good massage can help relax you or loosen a cramped muscle. Indians have always known and appreciated the benefits of massage. That is the reason that babies are given massage right from the time they are a few weeks old. Head massage, oil baths, body massage – these have been practised from ancient times and have become popular lately as people are rediscovering the efficacy of massage.

If you are feeling too stressed and burnt out, go for a good body massage and see the difference it makes to your condition. Even a good head massage or foot massage can make a whole world of difference. Oriental countries like Thailand and Malaysia have popularised the concept of massage as a relaxing therapy. Ayurvedic massage in Kerala is drawing tourists in hordes. Most spas and health farms have introduced massage in their treatments. Foot massage or reflexology is also a therapy that is creating renewed interest amongst people, for its restful benefits.

What is more important is that massage releases the feel-good chemicals called endorphins that elevate mood and fight depression. These are the same chemicals that are realised in our body when we walk. These feel-good chemicals automatically fight fatigue and low-energy making us feel more buoyant and happy.

Credible studies are starting to show that massage may even enhance immune response, perhaps by encouraging the brain to release fewer stress hormones and/or more natural painkillers into the bloodstream.

Massage is actually a much broader term that is defined as any kind of 'systematic manipulation of the soft tissues of the body' (such as muscle and connective tissue). Manipulation can mean any combination of rubbing, kneading, slapping, tapping, rolling, pressing or jostling, as long as the goal is to make you feel better.

Close to a hundred different techniques fit this definition of massage, most of which were developed in the past 20 years. Many massage therapists use a variety of these techniques.

Pros and Cons

While it is helpful to know what benefits can be reaped from massage therapy, it is equally important to be aware of the possible harm that may come about.

Pros

Massage increases the muscle tone and improves stamina, vitality and virility. It also helps activate digestion and the elimination of the body's waste like sweat, urine, stool, etc. Besides helping you relax, soothing sore muscles, reducing some kinds of swelling and improving general well-being, massage therapy of one sort or another may also help with hypertension, burns, chronic pain (including from arthritis, backaches and migraines), rashes and other skin conditions, addictions, depression, stress and pain of labour, asthma and attention deficit hyperactivity disorder (ADHD).

It can also alleviate depression and boost self-esteem in people with eating disorders; improve growth and development in premature babies; reduce pain and water retention in women with premenstrual syndrome (PMS); raise blood sugar levels in kids with diabetes; and possibly even boost immune function in people with HIV or cancer.

Massage is particularly useful in stress relief and loosening of muscles. It helps in promoting sound sleep and is highly relaxing.

Cons

While massage doesn't generally cause any harm, there are some precautions that can be followed in order to avoid any possible harm.

If you have a serious or chronic illness, don't undertake massage without first consulting a doctor. You should also generally avoid using massage on inflamed, burned, or otherwise injured areas. And because massage works by promoting blood flow, it can potentially spread certain problems throughout your body.

You should almost always avoid massage therapy if you have an infection, cancer, swelling (oedema) or a blood clot (except under the supervision of a highly skilled physician). People with high blood pressure, an enlarged liver or spleen, or peptic ulcers should also avoid abdominal massages. And pregnant women should stick to well-trained, professional massage therapists who are familiar with pregnancy massage.

Self-Massage

Self-massage can be done on a daily basis by almost anyone, in order to maintain good health and practise ongoing prevention. The massage should be done with the oil that is appropriate for one's constitution.

It is a simple procedure that does not require great skills but can be a very effective way to reduce stress and insomnia.

It is preferable to warm the oil before using it. Usually different oils are used for the head and the body. Oils that are cool in potency should be used for applying on the head, while those that are warm in nature should be used for general body massage.

The massage is done with gentle strokes of the fingers, thumbs and palms. Skill is more important than power in this case. Patting, gentle rubbing, soft squeezing and vibrations are the best way to stimulate the circulation and relax the muscles.

First, apply the oil on top of the head and massage it in for a minute. For massaging the scalp use the fingertips. Then massage the face, front and back of the neck and head with the palm.

Take the oil suitable for body massage and start massaging the external ear by holding the right ear lobe in the thumb and index finger. Use the tip of the index finger to massage the innermost part of the ear. Repeat the same procedure for the left ear.

The arms should be massaged with back and forth movements while the joints need circular movements. Use gentle, circular movements on the abdomen and chest region.

Lastly, apply oil on the lower limbs using long, strong strokes. The soles of the feet should be massaged with firm hands. Leave the oil on the body at least for 15 to 20 minutes before taking a warm bath or shower.

A Relaxing Massage

Work on your 'trigger points'. These are the aching nodules caused by stress leading to a muscle spasm, reduction of blood flow to the area and build up of lactic acid. Using finger pressure, you can disperse the lactic acid, get the blood flowing again and relax the muscle. Use a firm finger pressure, (as firm as you can bear) and hold each press for a slow count of ten. Don't use massage oil.

- Use the third and fourth finger of each hand to press the crown of the head.
- Using your thumb, press at one inch intervals along the base of the skull, first one side and then the other.

- Using the left-hand fingers, squeeze right side of neck, then use right-hand fingers on left side of neck.
- Use right-hand fingers to press the muscle at the back of the left shoulder in the triangle between the collarbone and shoulder blade. You will immediately know when you have found the right spot! Repeat on the other side.
- Move fingers slightly further in towards spine and press again. Repeat on the other side.

RECAP

- Massage is one of the best ways to relax fatigued muscles. It de-stresses and detoxifies them.
- Massage heals, rejuvenates, energises and relaxes all muscles in the body. It is also one of the most effective stress-fighting techniques that can be adopted without much expense or effort.
- Massage can make you feel upbeat because it seems to affect almost everything your body does.
- Massage improves circulation, busts stress, relieves pain, lowers heart rate and blood pressure, reduces swelling, strengthens muscles, promotes healing, restores motion to joints and accelerates basic bodily functions.
- Massage enhances immune response, perhaps by encouraging the brain to release fewer stress hormones.
- It catalyses the brain to release natural painkillers into the bloodstream.
- Everyone can do basic massage at home. One does not need to visit a spa or a massage parlour

for a simple, relaxing massage, although it is definitely much more relaxing when someone does it for you.

The Relaxing Breath

Surprising as it may seem, we have forgotten the art of breathing. Stress has robbed us of the purifying breath that our body requires in order to function at its best.

We breathe in nearly 500 cu ft of air per day. Our breath is automatic and consistent, yet so many times we find ourselves straining to breathe, especially when we're tensed up. Breathing is important for two reasons. It is the only means to supply our body and its various organs with oxygen, which is vital for our survival. The second function of breathing is that it is one means to get rid of waste products and toxins from the body.

Oxygen is the most vital nutrient for our bodies. It is essential for the efficient working of the brain, nerves, glands and internal organs. We can do without food for weeks and without water for days, but without oxygen, we will die within a few minutes. If the brain does not get proper supply of this essential nutrient, it will result in the degradation of all vital organs in the body.

The brain requires more oxygen than any other organ. If it doesn't get enough, the result is mental sluggishness, negative thoughts and depression, and eventually, vision and hearing decline. We know how to breathe. It is something that occurs to us automatically, spontaneously, naturally.

We are breathing even when we are not aware of it. So it seems foolish to think that one can be told how to breathe. Yet, one's breathing becomes modified and restricted in various ways, not just momentarily, but habitually. We develop unhealthy habits without being aware of it. Without realising that we are assuming an unhealthy posture, most of us tend to slouch when we sit or even when we stand. The result is diminished lung capacities since the lungs can't expand fully.

Stress seriously impacts our breathing. When our muscles are taut with tension, our breathing becomes shallow and rapid. We cannot take in sufficient oxygen nor do we eliminate sufficient carbon dioxide. As we continue breathing shallowly, it becomes a habit to do so. As a result, our bodies are oxygen starved, and a toxic build-up occurs. Every cell in the body requires oxygen, and our level of vitality is just a product of the health of all the cells.

Shallow breathing does not exercise the lungs enough, so they lose some of their function, causing a further reduction in vitality. Quick shallow breathing results in oxygen starvation, which leads to reduced vitality, premature ageing, poor immune system and myriad other problems. Our resistance to disease is reduced, because oxygen is essential for healthy cells. This means we catch more colds and develop other ailments more easily. Lack of sufficient oxygen to the cells is a major contributing factor to cancer, heart disease and strokes.

Why Is Our Breath Fast and Shallow?

There are several reasons for this.

- We are in a hurry most of the time. Our movements and breathing follow this pattern.
- The increasing stress of modern living makes us breathe more quickly and less deeply.
- We get emotional too easily. We get excited and angry easily, and suffer almost constantly from anxiety and worry. These negative emotional states affect the rate of breathing, causing it to be fast and shallow.
- Modern technology and automation has reduced our need for physical activity. There is less need to breathe deeply, so we develop the shallow-breathing habit.
- We spend more time indoors, and there is an

increased exposure to pollutants. As a result, the body instinctively inhales less air to protect itself from pollution. Those who spend more time outdoors do not suffer from shallow breathing.

As we go through life, these bad breathing habits we picked up become part of our life. Unless we take strong steps to reverse these habits, we can suffer permanent problems. The good news is that these are reversible. The bad news is that before we can change these habits we should recognise and accept that our behaviour needs to be changed.

There are three basic types of breathing.

1. Clavicular Breathing is the most shallow and worst possible type. The shoulders and collarbone are raised while the abdomen is contracted during inhalation. Maximum effort is made, but a minimum amount of oxygen is obtained in this kind of breathing
2. Thoracic Breathing is done with the rib muscles expanding the rib cage, and is the second type of incomplete breathing.
3. Deep Abdominal Breathing is the best kind of breathing, for it brings air to the lowest and largest part of the lungs. This kind of breathing is slow and deep, and the diaphragm is put to full use.

Actually, none of these types is complete. A full Yogic breath combines all three, beginning with a deep breath and continuing the inhalation through the intercostal and clavicular areas.

The Abdominal Breathing

To get the feel of proper diaphragmatic breathing, wear loose clothing and lie on the back. Place the hand on the upper abdomen, where the diaphragm is located. Breathe in and out slowly. The abdomen should expand outward as you inhale and contract as you exhale. Try to get the feeling of this motion.

Yogic Breathing

Once you feel proficient in the practice of the abdominal breathing, you will be ready to learn the Full Yogic Breathing. Breathe in slowly; expand the abdomen, then the rib cage, and finally the upper portion of the lungs. Then, breathe out in the same manner, letting the abdomen cave in as you exhale. This is the Yogic complete breath.

Deep Breathing Benefits

Deep breathing allows more oxygen into the lungs leading to an improvement in the quality of the blood. This aids in the elimination of toxins from the system, improving digestion and assimilation of food. The digestive organs such as the stomach receive more oxygen, and hence, operate more efficiently.

The brain requires three times more oxygen than the rest of the body. Increased supply of oxygen in the body leads to better functioning of the nervous system, including the brain, spinal cord, nerve centres and nerves. This, in turn, leads to improved health of the whole body. There is a rejuvenation of the glands, especially the pituitary and pineal glands. This has far-reaching effects on our well-being.

The skin becomes smoother and there are less facial wrinkles due to the enhanced oxygen supply in the body.

The movements of the diaphragm during the deep breathing exercise massage the abdominal organs – the stomach, small intestine, liver and pancreas. The upper movement of the diaphragm also massages the heart. This stimulates the blood circulation in these organs. The lungs become healthy and powerful, a good insurance against respiratory problems.

Deep, slow, yoga breathing reduces the workload for the heart. The result is a more efficient and stronger heart that operates better and lasts longer. It also means reduced blood pressure and low probability of heart disease.

Deep, slow breathing assists in weight control. If you are overweight, the extra oxygen burns up the excess fat more efficiently. If you are underweight, the extra oxygen feeds the starving tissues and glands.

Deep breathing encourages a complete relaxation of the mind and body. Slow, deep, rhythmic breathing causes a reflex stimulation of the parasympathetic nervous system, which results in a reduction in the heart rate and relaxation of the muscles. These two factors cause a reflex relaxation of the mind, since the mind and body are interdependent.

In addition, oxygenation of the brain tends to normalise brain function, reducing excessive anxiety levels. The breathing exercises cause an increase in the elasticity of the lungs and rib cage, which creates an increased breathing capacity.

As the breath finds its way through the open channels of the body, the mind does so as well, by weaving itself into the strands of thought and sensation that flow through the body. When the breath is free, the mind is free. When the breath is allowed to move naturally, the mind settles into itself. When the mind relaxes, the tongue and palette become spacious, the roof of the mouth lifts and hollows, and the central core of the body opens up.

The Secret of Vitality

One of the secrets of vitality and rejuvenation is a purified blood stream. The quickest and most effective way to purify the blood stream is by taking in extra supplies of oxygen from the air we breathe. Oxygen clears up the waste products (toxins) in the body, as well as recharging the body's batteries. By purifying the blood stream, every part of the body benefits along with the mind. The complexion becomes clearer and brighter and wrinkles will begin to fade away. In short, rejuvenation will begin to occur.

Scientists have known for a long time that there exists a strong connection between respiration and mental states. Improper breathing produces diminished mental ability. It is well known that mental tensions produce restricted breathing. A normally sedentary person, when confronted with a perplexing problem, tends to lean forward, draw his arms together, and bend his head down. All these body postures result in reduced lung capacity.

We become fatigued from the decreased circulation of the blood and from the decreased availability of oxygen for the blood because we have almost stopped breathing. As our duties, responsibilities and their attendant problems become more demanding, we develop habits of forgetting to breathe.

Shallow breathing does not exercise the lungs enough, so they lose some of their function, causing a further reduction in vitality.

The Vital Breath

Start by learning correct breathing techniques when lying down, alone and without distractions. Once you have mastered the technique, it can be practised in any position, anywhere – eventually it will become a habit.

1. Wear loose, comfortable clothes and lie on your back, preferably on the floor, using a mat, or on a bed if you are not comfortable on the floor.
2. Place both your hands on the lower edges of your ribs, with fingers nearly touching.
3. Sigh deeply and relax your body.
4. Breathe in deeply and smoothly through your nostrils. As you do so, you should be able to feel your diaphragm pulling out and down, your stomach rising and your ribs expanding upwards and outwards.
5. Hold the breath for a few seconds.
6. Now exhale completely and smoothly. This requires no muscular activity since all that happens is that the diaphragm and the muscles of the chest let go. Try to ensure that all the air that you inhaled is

expelled. The ribs collapse down and move inwards while the stomach lowers.

7. Repeat three or four times, then relax and breathe naturally for a few minutes, before starting the sequence once again.

Note:

- The shoulders should remain stationary during breathing. Many people, especially women, breathe solely into their upper lobes by raising and loweing their shoulders. This does not give the body an ade quate supply of oxygen and is a common symptom of stress.
- If you feel heady and faint during the breathing exercises, relax and breathe naturally for a few minutes – the sensation will pass quickly. The heady feeling is the result of the brain receiving an unusually large amount of oxygen.

While Sitting

- Make sure you are sitting comfortable with your spine straight.
- Relax your shoulders and place your hands loosely on your lap.
- Breathe using the same basic method as for lying down.
- Feel the air filling your lungs, right down to the bottom lobes.
- Check your shoulders – they should not be moving up and down.
- If you feel that you are not filling your lungs fully, place your hands on the bottom edge of the ribs, and over the stomach and see that your ribs and stomach are expanding fully under your fingers as you breathe in.

- Continue to breathe in this manner a few times until you are able to experience the right movements and then return your hands to your lap.
- After a while you will be able to breathe correctly in a natural manner.

While Walking

- Walk at a steady pace, letting your hands swing loosely by your side.
- Breathe in deeply – as in the basic method – for a certain number of paces, hold the breath for half that number and breathe out gradually for the same number. Find which number of paces feels right for you.
- Maintain the rhythm and repeat the exercise five times. Then relax and breathe naturally.
- Repeat the whole exercise a few times during each walk.

The Healing Breath

This method of healing in used in all branches of eastern medicine, though not in orthodox western medicine. It involves breathing in the chi, as Chinese and Japanese medicine calls the 'life force', or the prana, as Indian medicine names it, into the lungs and visualising it flowing from them first into the solar plexus and then to the area to be healed. During exhalation, the disease is visualised flowing out of the body.

A Re-Energising Exercise

These two exercises in breathing will first perform a releasing function on your body and mind and then recharge them. The second exercise is especially structured to boost your vitality, but it should be used sparingly to prevent hyperventilation.

- Breathe in deeply through an open mouth and sigh out with a relaxed throat. Your upper back widens during inhaling and releases on exhaling. Don't worry if you yawn; it's your body's homeostatic mechanism correcting the oxygen and carbon dioxide balance.
- Open your mouth wide, inhale deeply and let the air out in a big 'hah'. Repeat a few times quickly. If you feel light-headed, breathe normally through your nose.
- Tingling in your mouth or fingers is a normal reaction to shifting levels of oxygen and carbon dioxide.

A Stress-Releasing Exercise

This exercise is particularly useful, since it only takes a few minutes and can be performed anywhere, at any time.

- Stand up with your hands hanging loosely by your side.
- Breathe in slowly through your nostrils, tensing all your muscles at the same time.
- Hunch your shoulders up to your ears, clench your hands as hard as possible, tighten your stomach muscles, clench your buttocks and raise yourself up on to tiptoe.
- Hold this position to the count of five. Fix your eye on something straight ahead to help you balance.
- Slowly breathe out through your nostrils and at the same time relax all your muscles, so that by the time you have fully exhaled, your shoulders are down, your hands are loose, your stomach is relaxed, and your knees are slightly bent.
- Repeat five times.

Alternate Nose Breathing

This breathing technique is recommended for calming the spirit and the mind. The sun and moon are seen here as symbols of the positive and the negative, and this technique shows you how to inhale the positive energy of the sun and exhale the negative waste products of the body.

- Sit in an upright position or in a cross-legged position, on the floor. If you find it difficult to do so, sit on a straight-back chair.
- Pinch your nostrils shut with your right hand, the thumb closing the right nostril and the index and middle finger closing the left nostril. Only gentle pressure is needed, so do not pinch too hard.
- Breathe through your mouth as you practise opening and closing the nostrils alternately.
- When you have learnt how to do this, inhale deeply and slowly as for the basic method through your right nostril – keep the left nostril firmly closed.
- Hold for the amount of time it took you to inhale – though not if it feels uncomfortable.
- Exhale gradually through your left nostril again for the same length of time it took to inhale. The comparative ratio for these three motions – breathing in, holding, then breathing out – is therefore 1:1:1. This rhythm can take a while to master, but eventually, you become adept at it. Experts in yoga use a ratio of 1:4:2. It is good enough if you are able to maintain a ratio of 1:2:2.
- Breathe in this manner at least five times.
- Reverse the process by using the left nostril to inhale and the right nostril to exhale.
- Repeat five times.
- Breathe twice through both nostrils deeply and fully.

- As you breathe deeply, you will feel your body relaxing completely and the tension disappearing.

The De-Stressing Breath

The more stressed out we are, the tighter we hold ourselves, especially in the jaw, chest and diaphragm. If we breathe deeply, the oxygen flows, and we can think and feel more clearly.

This exercise will help you de-stress and unwind.

- Sit cross-legged on the floor, or in a chair with your feet flat on the ground, head straight and chin parallel to the floor.
- Inhale slowly through your nose, filling your abdomen, ribs and chest. Then blow out steadily though puckered lips until your lungs are empty.
- Breathe in again, feeling your torso muscles move like bellows. Visualise yourself expelling the tension from your body.

RECAP

- Breathing is the only means to supply our bodies and its various organs with oxygen, which is vital for our survival. It is also a means to get rid of waste products and toxins from the body.
- The brain requires more oxygen than any other organ. If it doesn't get enough, the result is mental sluggishness, negative thoughts and depression, and eventually, vision and hearing decline.
- Stress seriously impacts our breathing. When our muscles are taut with tension, our breathing becomes shallow and rapid. There is insufficient intake of oxygen, and elimination of carbon dioxide is also inadequate.
- Oxygen clears up the waste products (toxins) in

the body, as well as recharges the body's batteries. It is essential to our cells to increase our resistance to disease.

- Scientists have found a strong connection between respiration and mental states. Improper breathing produces diminished mental ability.
- Increased supply of oxygen in the body leads to better functioning of the nervous system, including the brain, spinal cord, nerve centres and nerves.
- There is a rejuvenation of the glands, especially the pituitary and pineal glands. This has far-reaching effects on our well-being.
- The skin becomes smoother and there are less facial wrinkles due to the enhanced oxygen supply in the body.

Vigour and Vitality

Vitality is described as persistent energy, vigour or liveliness in the lexicon. How do we find this persistent energy? Where does it come from?

When there is fatigue within and without, vitality seems to be unattainable. Vitality comes from the body's energy resources. It comes to us from potent environmental sources like the sun, our food and water, and the air we breathe. These energy sources, when transformed into body energy, become the vitality that keeps us vibrant and alive. The more vitality you have, the stronger you are, the greater your physical well-being, and the more inspired you feel.

The concept of boosting vitality through natural means is one that the great majority of people tend to ignore. Vitality is not sold on counters, despite the claim from many pharmaceutical companies. It comes from the optimum use of the naturally available sources of energy, in the environment. The right diet, efficient breathing, regular exercise, sufficient water intake, all promote vitality.

The fundamental elements of a healthy lifestyle, particularly on those areas of living that are within our direct control, need to be examined in order to bring about vitality and healthy living. The most obvious way of enhancing our well-being is by paying attention to our diet, getting sufficient exercise and incorporating proper breathing and relaxation techniques in our life.

Vitality, however, is more than simple physical health. It encompasses many more factors like emotions and mental happiness. Even the robust constitution doesn't grant unlimited energy because that comes from a well-balanced and fine-tuned body and mind. Fatigued minds are not full of vitality. Happiness and contentment play a vital role in achieving enduring energy. For instance, if you are feeling depressed or unhappy, will your energy level be undiminished even if you are at the peak of physical health?

How Does One Attain Indefatigable Energy?

The problems faced by people today, have become much more complex than before. Society has become more complex. Somehow, the concept of economic 'success' has replaced the traditional values of human bonding, of communication with nature, of a deep knowledge of life, and of what is important in sustaining life and cultivating wisdom. Economic success has replaced what brings true happiness, and it has done so at the inconceivable expense of the land and the environment that supports life. Technological 'success' has been at the unfathomable expense of the people, of whole cultures, and ways of life born out of the wisdom of the ages, which, for centuries, supported mankind, high cultural expression, and supreme spiritual life, especially among the people of Asian countries.

According to George Oshawa, the person who discovered the macrobiotic way of life, we have seven stages of judgment or thinking ability. The first stage is the subconscious mind. This is the consciousness of the autonomic nervous system, the sympathetic and parasympathetic nervous systems.

The second stage of thinking is sensorial, that is, judgments made using the sense organs that distinguish colour, shape, distance, sound, smell, taste and touch. This stage of nerve function is instantaneous and spontaneous and does not require the consciousness of higher brain function. At this stage, there is no time for thinking; reactions are like reflexes, they operate instantly. Therefore, this stage of thinking exists in even the simplest creatures such as insects, fish and snails. However, this stage of judgment also exists in more complex creatures such as mammals, including humans. In humans, however, those sensorial reflections are slower and less sharp than those of simpler creatures since humans, with their higher brain functions, are always thinking.

However, some humans do not use their higher brain functions to think, but use them only for sensorial reflection. They behave with emotion, but not with reason. Their goals in life focus on nice clothes, better cars, better houses, tasty foods, better sex, and other conveniences and comforts.

Often, at the end of these pleasures are financial difficulties, sicknesses, arguments, anger, resentment and jealousy. Since those people live according to reflex senses, they cannot overcome or change difficulties in their life. In order to change difficulties, to happiness, we need endurance, which requires more than the sensorial level or stage of consciousness.

One who lives according to the senses does not use the higher brain functions, which require endurance. Therefore, when they encounter difficulties, they are desperate, disappointed and unhappy. So, the first condition of character to be able to live a happy life is endurance.

Someone who has no endurance cannot overcome difficulties. To overcome difficulties one has to try hard, especially after failing a few times, and never give up, to be able to transform unhappiness to happiness.

If you want to be happy, don't try to be perfect or always first. This desire, taken to an extreme, can create enormous stress in your life and can lead to arrogance. This stress and arrogance can create an emotional quicksand that will rob you of good quality energy and will sap your endurance.

Life goals pursued for mundane reasons like money, power or status are likely to make you unhappy.

Find your purpose and create meaning in your life because a person with a meaningful existence will never lack vitality.

AFFIRMATIONS FOR RELAXATION

Affirmation can be likened to a flower seed in a garden, which needs tending to make sure it survives, and the negative responses are weeds in the garden that must be uprooted to allow space to the seed. Affirmations help heal suppressed material and promote integration. They are a positive application of creative thought.

Affirmations are those powerful words which, when repeatedly uttered, create positive energy and strong vibrations of the thought process. They bring about success and self-confidence by raising the thoughts to a surreal stratum. Whatever we utter goes out into the atmosphere, and we build our own aura by these strong vibrations. Whatever goes from you will return to you at some time or other. This is a natural law, and so in using our thoughts and speech power in a positive direction, we can build up a very powerful force for the highest good, which in turn attracts more subtle forces of the same quality in the spiritual realms. This generates tremendous vibrations of protection, strength, upliftment and power in our lives and the lives of those with whom we come in contact.

Repeated uttering of affirmations help the minds to attain a positive attitude that can overcome all kinds of weaknesses. The power of thought is fuelled by emotion and feelings. Affirmations are the resonate forms of the thoughts that otherwise lie hidden beneath a veneer of doubt and uncertainty. We harbour all kinds of thoughts in our minds, some conscious and some unconscious. Some are negative while others are positive. Our ambitions, wishes, dreams lie embedded within these thoughts and when we speak them aloud, we create vibrations of a positive kind that make it possible for those wishes and dreams to take shape and form.

Affirmations are like the charger of your mobile. If you do not charge the handset, you cannot use it. Likewise, positive words repeated sincerely charge up the subconscious mind with their vibrations, making the mind much stronger.

You may find it useful to counter negative thoughts with positive affirmations. You can use affirmations to build confidence and change negative behaviour patterns into positive ones. You can base affirmations on clear, rational assessments of fact, and use them to undo the damage that negative thinking may have done to your self-confidence.

Examples of affirmations are:

- I can do this.
- I can achieve my goals.
- I am completely myself and people will like me for myself.
- I am completely in control of my life.
- I am relaxed.
- I am rejuvenated.
- I am absolutely stress free.

You can coin your own personal affirmations and make them your code, to be used whenever you feel stressed or low. Coining these codes for each occasion can be immensely beneficial. You may have as many as a hundred affirmations to be used whenever you wish.

A positive affirmation can lift your life and help you achieve your goal. Such an affirmation sends your message to the cosmic aura, and the cosmos listens and responds in positive manifestation of your desires. Affirmations can be used like mantras. A frequently-repeated phrase directs our mind on a course of our choosing, and it takes up mental bandwidth. We can only hold a limited amount of content in your conscious mind at a time. A mantra or an affirmation takes up space and crowds out less-desirable thoughts, such as worry and negative self-talk. Since those negative thoughts are unhelpful, we serve ourselves better by choosing thoughts that calm us and move us toward our goals.

The affirmation must be a dedicated belief. They work best when you free yourself from your limiting insecurities and judgements and replace them with beliefs that you have unlimited potential.

Getting Started

- You should have a positive goal... Spend a few minutes in a quiet and relaxing environment. Think about what you want from life. Is it to do with relationships? Or career, self-love, direction, improved health or energy?

  If you can't think of a goal, do you have a negative nagging thought that you could turn around? For example, instead of thinking 'I am fat' every morning, you could change this around to 'I am healthy and energised'.
- Believe without fear that your desire will come true. Know that you truly deserve what you are asking for, without guilt.
- Let your affirmation go with love and trust. To focus intensely on the affirmation after establishing it will stifle it. Simply return to the affirmation gently once a day to boost your power. Gentle, successive sessions will have a compound effect.
- Always create your affirmation in present tense. Place yourself in the situation as you want it – to talk about it in future tense will mean your desire is always waiting to happen.

- Use only positive words. The cosmos does not acknowledge words such as 'not' or 'don't'. So, instead of saying 'I am not poor', say 'I have enough money for all that I need.'
- Indulge yourself in the moment as your affirmation sinks in. Then, let it go. By not dwelling on how the change might show up, you let the cosmos work her magic naturally.
- Keep your affirmation short and specific. Focus on one key element at a time, without the clutter of many desires all at once.
- Repetition of your affirmation means your desire can sink into every fibre of your being, settling naturally into your way of life.

Making Affirmations Work

- Write the affirmation by hand. Write it hundreds of times, until the affirmation has imprinted itself into your subconscious mind.
- The first thing in the morning or the last thing at night, when you are your most relaxed, can be making affirmations. Our minds more easily absorb behaviour-changing patterns then.
- Say your affirmation into a recording device and play it back often. Play it as you are falling asleep. The more often you repeat the affirmation, the more likely it is that your mind will accept the idea as truth and begin to behave accordingly. Be persistent.
- Put some emotion into it. The more you align your feelings and the thought, the more powerful the exercise will be.
- Visualise the result. Use words and imagery together with feeling to bring more of your brain into the creative process.

- Your affirmation may affirm something that does not exist at this moment, but the goal should be conceivable. If what you affirm is too far out of your frame of reference, your mind may resist it. On the other hand, don't be afraid to stretch.
- Once you have focused your thought, take action.
- Generally, work with any single affirmation a maximum of two weeks. This isn't long engougħ for staleness to set in, but long enough for the message to sink to every corner of your self-perception.

Laughter and Relaxation

To laugh often and much;
To win the respect of intelligent people and the affection of children;
To earn the appreciation of honest critics and endure the betrayal of false friends;
To appreciate beauty;
To find the best in others;
To leave the world a bit better, whether by a healthy child, a garden path or a redeemed social condition;
To know that even one life has breathed easier because you have lived.
This is to have succeeded.

—Ralph Waldo Emerson

Everyone looks for a sense of humour in the companion. Whether it is while seeking a lifemate or a friend, humour is one ingredient that is considered vital for a relationship. It is clinically proven to be effective in combating stress, although the exact mechanism is not known. Experts say a good laugh relaxes tense muscles, speeds more oxygen into your system and lowers your blood pressure. So tune into your favourite sitcom on television. Read a funny book. Call a friend and chuckle for a few minutes. It even helps to force a laugh once in a while. You'll find your stress melting away almost instantly.

Laughter therapy is turning out to be one of the most successful stress busters. Laughter is the best medicine, so says ancient wisdom, and it is truly so. A hundred belly laughs is the aerobic equivalent of ten minutes on a rowing-exercise machine. According to researchers, laughter increases blood flow and contracts the abdominal muscles. Stress hormones can trigger irregularity in the heartbeats, which can harm the heart. Laughter can ebb the release of those stress hormones. Laughter oxygenates your body, helping you to feel more energetic and sharp. Laughter improves both circulation and metabolism. That is not all – laughter releases endorphins in the body, which are natural painkillers.

The emotions and moods we experience directly affect our immune system. A sense of humour allows us to perceive and appreciate the incongruities of life and provides moments of joy and delight.

Share funny episodes with your spouse so that both can relieve stress as well improve communication between the two of you.

Dr Lee Berk and fellow researcher Dr Stanley Tan at Loma Linda University School of Medicine found that laughter stimulates the immune system, offsetting the immuno-suppressive effects of stress.

Humour gives us a different perspective on our problems. If we can make light out of the situation, it no longer threatens us. Because we have already discounted its effect. With such an attitude of detachment, we feel a sense of self-protection and control in our environment. According to Bill Cosby, 'If you can laugh at it, you can survive it.'

It's sometimes difficult to force a laugh in tense situations. But that's precisely when you need it most. One trick for finding humour in the worst of situations is to blow things absolutely and ridiculously out of proportion. When your scenario reaches the point of absurdity, you begin to smile. The situation is put in perspective and then you can calm down.

Laughter decreases 'stress' hormones that constrict blood vessels and suppress immune activity. In a study, a group of people exposed to humour showed remarkable decrease in the stress hormone levels.

The levels of epinephrine were lower in the group both in anticipation of humour and after exposure to humour. Epinephrine levels remained down throughout the experiment.

In addition, dopamine levels were also decreased. Dopamine is involved in the 'fight or flight response' and is associated with elevated blood pressure.

Experts believe that, when used as an adjunct to conventional care, laughter can reduce pain and aid the healing process. For one thing, laughter offers a powerful distraction from pain.

In a study published in the *Journal of Holistic Nursing,* patients were told one-liners after surgery and before painful medication was administered. Those exposed to humour perceived less pain when compared to patients who didn't get a dose of humour as part of their therapy.

Perhaps, the biggest benefit of laughter is that it is free and has no known negative side effects.

SHAVASANA

Shavasana or the Corpse Pose is an excellent posture that can be used for total relaxation. This single asana can help in the management of hypertension, anxiety, exhaustion, insomnia and other stress-related ailments. Yet, it requires no special equipment and is one of the easiest asanas to perform. Its efficacy lies in the fact that it brings the mind to the Alpha state, which is the key to creativity and good health. Shavasana brings about the calm state of mind that is excellent for visualisation and relaxation.

This pose can also be practised any time when one requires a few minutes of total rest and relaxation. All you need is a quiet place and solitude. For greater effectivity one can incorporate a technique that requires the observation of the breath. Observing the rhythm of breath and chanting a mantra can relax the mind completely.

All one has to do is to let the muscles relax, feel the circulation of prana throughout the system and be attuned to cosmic energies. Shavasana calms the brain and helps relieve stress and mild depression.

How to Do It

1. Lie down on your back, in a quiet place. Place the arms beside the body, palms upturned. Keep heels slightly apart.
2. Breathe slowly and deeply, feeling a sense of calm relaxation come over your whole body. Concentrate on loosening all tensions.

The following variation will increase your ability to relax:

1. Inhale slowly and deeply through the nostrils and tense the ankles, feet and toes. Hold the breath while you tighten the muscles. Exhale and relax.
2. Slowly inhale and contract the kneecaps, calves, ankles, feet and toes. Hold and tighten the muscles.
3. Exhale and relax.
4. Slowly inhale, contracting all the muscles of the abdomen, pelvic area, hips, thighs, kneecaps, calves, ankles, feet and toes.
5. Hold the breath and tighten the muscles.
6. Exhale and relax.
7. Inhale deeply. Tense the neck, shoulders, arms and elbows, wrists, hands and fingers, chest muscles, down to the toes. Hold and tense.
8. Exhale and relax.
9. Inhale and contract the scalp, the tiny muscles of the face, the forehead; squint the eyes, wrinkle the nose and mouth, tighten the tongue, constrict the throat and tighten the whole body.
10. Hold and feel the increasing tension.
11. Exhale and relax.
12. Now, let the tension leave the body slowly and melt

into the floor. You will experience a feeling of heaviness. Enjoy the support of the floor.

13. With sharpened senses, you will experience the tingling of the circulation of blood and an emotional calm.
14. In addition to quietening the physical body in Shavasana, it's also necessary to pacify the sense organs. Wilfully soften the root of the tongue, the wings of the nose, the channels of the inner ears, and the skin of the forehead, especially around the bridge of the nose between the eyebrows.
15. Let the eyes sink to the back of the head, then turn them downward to gaze at the heart. Release your brain to the back of the head.
16. Stay in this pose for 5–10 minutes.
17. To exit, first roll gently with an exhalation onto the right side. Take 2 or 3 breaths. With another exhalation press your hands against the floor and lift your torso, dragging your head slowly after. The head should always come up last.

In Shavasana, we let go of any particular breathing technique and simply allow the breath to move through its inherent inhaling and exhaling pattern. As the breath finds its way through the open channels of the body, the mind does so as well, by weaving itself into the strands of thought and sensation that flow through the body. When the breath is free, the mind is free. When the breath is allowed to move naturally, the mind settles into itself. When the mind relaxes, the tongue and palette become spacious, the roof of the mouth lifts and hollows and the central core of the body opens up.

RECAP

- Vitality is described as persistent energy, vigour or liveliness in the lexicon. It comes to us from sources like the sun, our food and water, and the air we breathe.

- These energy sources, when transformed into body energy, become the vitality that keeps us vibrant and alive. The more vitality you have, the stronger you are, the greater your physical well-being, and the more inspired you feel.
- Affirmations are those powerful words which, when repeatedly uttered, create positive energy and strong vibrations of the thought process.
- Affirmations can be used very effectively to produce positive thoughts and mental strength.
- Laughter is one of the most significant stress relievers. It stimulates the immune system, offsetting the immuno-suppressive effects of stress.
- Laughing is aerobic, providing a workout for the diaphragm and increasing the body's ability to use oxygen.
- Laughter brings in positive emotions that can enhance – not replace – conventional treatments. Hence, it is another tool available to help fight the disease.
- Laughter can reduce pain and aid the healing process.
- Shavasana can help in the management of hypertension, anxiety, exhaustion, insomnia and other stress-related ailments.
- Shavasana brings about the calm state of mind that is excellent for visualisation and relaxation. It also helps relieve mild depression.

CHAPTER THREE

Mental Relaxation

Like water, which does not retain any impression of the waves that play on its bosom, the mind should remain calm at all times.

—Sri Sri Parmahansa Yoganand

Almost all spiritual teachers and experts preach about the benefits of relaxation, but to a layman relaxation is synonymous with physical repose. Few understand the meaning of perfect relaxation of the body and mind. Most of us learn to relax physically, but mental relaxation remains far from being achieved, because it is tougher to attain.

Mind is the greatest gift the Almighty has presented to us. It is also the most powerful element in our lives. At the same time it can become the biggest enemy when it is not in a relaxed state. By nature, mind is restless. It arouses a gamut of thoughts every moment - some good and some bad. In modern parlance, we term them as positive and negative. Jealousy, anger, greed and regret are emotions that generate negative energies, while love and compassion generate positive energy.

The positive energy is revitalising and rejuvenating, healthy and happy in nature. Negative energy is destructive and unhealthy in nature. These energies are very potent and can cause far-reaching repercussions, not only in our lives but also in the lives of people around us.

Although we all seek peace and harmony, we experience agitation, irritation, disharmony, suffering, and when one suffers from agitation, one does not keep this misery limited to oneself. One keeps spreading it to others as well. The agitation permeates the atmosphere around the unhappy person. As a result, everyone who comes into contact with him also becomes irritated, agitated.

What is the cause for this agitation and unhappy state of mind? When we begin generating negativity, we are bound to become agitated because of the negativity in our mind. A mental defilement or impurity cannot exist with peace and harmony.

How Does One Start Generating Negativity?

Shri Goenka, the great master of Vipassana, said, 'I become very unhappy when I find someone behaving in a way which I don't like, when I find something happening which I don't like. Unwanted things happen, and I create tension within myself. Wanted things do not happen; some obstacles come in the way, and again I create tension within myself; I start tying knots within myself. And throughout life, unwanted things keep on happening, wanted things may or may not happen, and this process or reaction, of tying knots - Gordian knots - makes the entire mental and physical structure so tense, so full of negativity that life becomes miserable.'

Most of us are restless because we want something more in life. The 'I want' syndrome does not allow us to relax. There is an interesting story about the limitless desires faced by human beings.

A beggar once approached a king and asked if he could give him enough to fill his begging bowl. The king laughed and said, 'That bowl is not big enough to hold the amount of money or jewels that I can give you.'

The beggar humbly bowed to the king and said, 'Sir, you must think before you promise to fill the bowl. Do you have enough?'

The king was angry. He ordered his minister to fill the beggar's bowl with jewels. The minister carried out the order but found that the bowl was still empty. No matter how many jewels he poured into it, the bowl just didn't fill up. At last he gave up.

The king fell at the feet of the beggar and cried, 'You are no ordinary mortal, and this is not an ordinary bowl. Who are you?'

The beggar smiled and said, 'This bowl is the representative of human heart, which is never satisfied. No matter how much is given to him, the human being does not feel content.'

Every one of us would like to control situations and to change the course of events to suit us. We all want to control – control situations, control people and events, control the happiness factor, and everything around us. Since we can't control anything other than ourselves, shouldn't we begin by controlling the mind?

A person who has learnt to control the mind becomes a yogi, so it may not be possible for all of us to control the mind. In fact, it is the toughest thing to do. But, we can try. The first step is to bring peace and a sense of relaxation to this highly disturbed and restless mind.

This is where relaxation comes in. Each of us can do ourselves a favour and bring a sense of relaxation to our troubled minds.

A relaxed mind does not skip from one chore to another without completing any. If you can 'switch off' your mind at the end of the day, you have a relaxed mind. Your mind is not relaxed if you worry about small things that don't bother other people, and again you are not relaxed if it doesn't take much to make you lose your temper. You definitely need mental relaxation if you find that people tell you things but they don't seem to register in your brain.

RELAXATION AND EMOTIONS

Emotions, as expressed and experienced by humans can be divided into two broad categories – the positive and the negative emotions. Positive emotions are fuelled by an underlying desire for enjoyment and unity. Positive emotions are pleasant – for instance, interest, enthusiasm, boredom, love, happiness, laughter, empathy, action, curiosity and contentment.

On the other hand, negative emotions like feelings of apathy, grief, fear, hatred, shame, blame, regret, resentment, anger, hostility and loneliness are fuelled by an underlying fear of the unknown.

It is interesting to note that several American psychologists have devised an independent theory claiming that there are eight basic emotions. These emotions, which can exist at various levels of intensity, are anger, fear, joy, sadness, acceptance, disgust, surprise, and interest or curiosity. They combine to form all other emotions, just as basic colours give rise to all other colours. In our country, we have long known that there are nine kinds of emotions or 'navarasa', so efficiently demonstrated by our bharatnatyam dancers.

This might of course lead you to believe that the negative emotions are just something to get rid of. That is not true. One needs to deal with the negative emotions and actually work at transforming them into something more useful and enjoyable.

Positive emotions give you energy, while negative emotions deplete your energy. When you are excited and happy and are interacting with people you love and enjoy, you sparkle with energy and enthusiasm, but when you are angry or depressed, or negative for any reason, you feel tired and frustrated, and eventually feel burned out. The negative emotions are useful as motivation for moving away from what one doesn't want. The positive emotions are useful as motivation for moving towards what one wants.

The trouble with emotions is that they affect our life in a significant manner. Physical ailments are just some of those effects. Most of our disagreeable emotions produce muscle tightness. For instance, if you have been suffering from a host of disagreeable thoughts for the entire day, you are likely to tighten up the muscles. And when you do that, aches are the result. One of the first places to show the tension is the group of muscles at the back of the neck, and the other is the group of muscles at the upper end of the oesophagus. When they squeeze down you feel a lump, and it becomes difficult to swallow. Severe tightening of these muscles result in acute stomach aches.

A good number of people with severe headaches have them because the blood vessel inside or outside the skull is squeezing down so hard from nervous excitation that it produces pain. Have you ever noticed how your palm begins to sweat and your heartbeat revs up when you are nervous. Whether it is an interview or the first date, these symptoms attack most of us with an amazing impact. It is our emotions that come into play during such stressful situations.

Statistics reveal that one third of those suffering from skin diseases are actually suffering because of toxic thoughts. These are produced by blood vessels in the skin reacting to anxiety, worry, disgust and other negative emotions. Each time the individual becomes upset or irritated or peeved, serum is actually squeezed out through the wall of the blood vessel and into the skin. The tissues become thickened with it. Finally the serum is pushed up through the surface of the skin where it becomes crusty and itchy resulting in neuro-dematitis.

There are endless examples of the effect of negative emotions on the body. The endocrine glands are also affected by stress and acute fear. The emotion sends a message to the adrenal glands to squeeze adrenalin into the blood stream. When that adrenalin hits the heart, the heart begins to thump. When it hits the blood vessels going into the brain, they narrow down and make you feel faint. You realise that emotions are not just about the thoughts – they transcend into our minds and bodies expressing themselves in headaches and other pains and ailments.

Your energy level depends largely on your emotions. Whether it is the negative or positive energy, there is a charging of your batteries. Initially, even the hatred you feel towards someone builds up negative energy. It fills up the emotional storage tank almost to the bursting point. But it is largely negative energy that causes damage to your body as well as mind. It saps and drains you unlike the positive energy, which is generated by positive thoughts and emotions.

Positive Emotions are High-Voltage Energy

Positive emotions can provide you with high-voltage energy. Suppose it takes a thousand units of physical energy to activate your body and you conserve this energy by doing little physical labour, you can convert it into emotional energy. But you would get just about a hundred units of emotional energy from the thousand units of physical one because emotional energy is a far more superior form of energy. This emotional energy is very valuable to us. We have the option of squandering it away with negative emotions, such as fear, doubt, anger and resentment or conserve this valuable energy for higher voltage spiritual energy.

As we move from the base physical energy to higher voltage emotional energy to still higher voltage spiritual energy, we are moving into a different plane altogether. If your energy is conserved at one level, your body continues to refine it into higher and better energy. Transforming the energies into the highest voltage will result in spiritual happiness and peace.

Negative emotions drain us of our valuable emotional and mental energy. What happens when we are angry? When a person is angry, he is burning up the glucose or sugar-based energy in the system, and is actually weak from an angry outburst. A common characteristic of very successful people is that they keep themselves calm much longer than the average person does. They are more relaxed, more genial and more in control of their emotions. They are aware that expressions of negative emotion deprive them of the energy they need to be effective in the more important things they do. As a result, successful people don't allow themselves to become upset or angry over little things, or even over large things. They remain objective and detached. They stand back and refuse to take things personally. They save their emotional energy for far more productive purposes.

The whole purpose of physical relaxation is to allow yourself to recharge your emotional and mental batteries, thereby improving the overall quality of your entire life.

There are three things you can do to step up your energy voltage.

- First, keep your thoughts away from the things and people that cause you stress and negative emotions.
- Second, preserve your emotional energy by staying calm and positive in difficult situations rather than allowing yourself to become upset or angry.
- Third, take ample time to rest completely, so you can recharge your physical and emotional batteries. The better rested you are, the more effective you will be.

Emotion Management

The more we learn about the mind–body connection, the more we realise the benefits of having a control over our emotions. Emotion management is not about denying the negative emotions or thoughts, it would be superhuman to do that, but to recognise and channelise them.

There are three important steps to managing the emotions:

- The first step is to recognise the negative emotions that hound your mind and defining the reasons they are there. There always are reasons for them to be there, in the first place. If you are constantly on the warpath, what is the reason for such behaviour?

- Once you have been able to recognise the reason, the next step would be to cure it. Like the doctor who first diagnoses and then cures the illness, you will cure your mind of the negative emotions.
- Curing negative emotions does not mean just ignoring their presence or trying to deny them. It simply means realising the futility of wasting the energies on such emotions and then wilfully converting them into positive thoughts.

Detoxification of Emotions

Toxic emotions are very harmful. They brutalise and scar the soul, upset the mind and cause physical ailments. Need I say more? We are all human, and negative thoughts are a normal process.

To become as perfect as a mortal being can become, we need to bring the mind, body and spirit into total harmony. Within our universe are both positive and negative energies. Positive energy is: light, goodness, kindness, love, patience, charity, hope, etc. Negative is: darkness, hatred, fear, unkindness, intolerance, selfishness, despair, discouragement, etc.

Hatred, anger, jealousy are as intricately woven into our psyche as love, affection, compassion and concern. Fear is an emotion that is a huge hurdle to living a more relaxed life. Fear is an emotion conjured up within us in response to perceived danger. Sometimes that danger is real, but often it is imagined.

Whether you fear public speaking or 'the future', heights or spiders, fear is extremely stressful. One of the best ways to control irrational fear is through a slow process of desensitisation. Build up your tolerance one step at a time. If you are terrified of heights, force yourself to stand a little above the ground and look down. Repeat affirmations like 'I have risen above the fear of heights.' Gradually, work your way to higher heights, using the same affirmation.

Another approach is to visualise yourself overcoming your fear in as much detail as possible. According to

Mark Twain, 'Do the thing you fear the most and the death of fear is certain.'

Accept Your Emotions

We are all in emotional chaos, most of the time. If we could resolve our feelings, we would be doing something very important. Most of us are taught to aim for higher consciousness, to become a loving and blissful person, but we are never taught how to handle the negative feelings within ourselves. The intelligent ones soon realise that there is work to be done on the emotional level, and that their growth will be limited until they do so. The emotional planes come before the spiritual planes. In our journey of consciousness, we must clear the planes in ascending order: physical, emotional, mental, intellectual and spiritual. If we aim for the 'spiritual' with no attention to feelings, we are bound to be unstable in our growth, and are likely to end up suppressing our feelings in the name of spirituality.

Another important realisation about feelings has been emerging strongly over the last six or eight years. More and more is being written about the connection between suppressed feelings and chronic poor health. Healing professionals are advocating the idea that in order to resolve health issues, people must resolve the emotional issues behind them. Awareness is growing that the unreleased and trapped negative emotional energy keeps building inside and eventually manifests in the physical.

When we repress our feelings, they show up in other self-destructive ways, including anger, rage, overeating, anorexia, drugs, alcohol, smoking or depression. No one can remain positive all the time. You are bound to have your share of negative as well as positive emotions. It is normal to feel bad, and express it. You will be emotionally healthier if you accept rather than deny the negatives.

All of us must have suffered from the feelings of resentment at some time or the other. When we were children, we might have resented a classmate who seemed to have the things we didn't have. As teenagers we might have resented the boy who got the girl we adored, and then as adults we might have resented colleagues who bypassed us in career. It is a part of life. Imagine what would happen if we tried to suppress our resentment. Resentment robs us of vital emotional energy but suppressed resentment makes us bankrupt.

Whenever you find yourself resenting someone, try to figure out why you resent him or her. Being objective about the point of resentment sometimes brings about a transformation. Do you realise that the person you resent may have his own grievances against you? The most awful fact about a negative emotion is that it generates more negativity around you. As you spread the negative energies and throw them into the atmosphere, it returns manifold to you. For instance, if you sow the seeds of hatred, you will certainly reap a bumper crop of hatred. Now it is up to you to use that crop or destroy it. Similarly, if you spread the positive energy of love around you, you will receive it with interest from all sides.

It is also a good idea to talk to a supportive person when you have doubts about the validity of your feelings, a person who will listen and reassure you of your right to feel bad. Consider the following questions and how they relate to the experiences of your own life: How will we be able to recognise joy if we have never felt sadness? How can we know fulfilment if we have never known loss? And how can we be human if we never feel?

Each soul has the capacity to be filled with love and eternal energy. Everything we do to show love is worthwhile: a smile, a word of encouragement and a small act of sacrifice. We grow by these actions. Not all people are lovable, but when we find someone difficult for us to love, it is often because they remind us of something within ourselves that we don't like. Let go of anger, hate, envy, bitterness and the refusal to forgive. These things destroy the spirit. Spiritual, physical and universal laws govern us all, and these laws were created to fulfil a purpose and all laws compliment each other. When we recognise these laws and learn to use their positive and negative forces, we will have access to power beyond our comprehension.

Positive and negative energies work in opposition to each other. When we internalise these energies, they become our servants. Positive attracts the positive and negative attracts negative. We have the choice to become either positive or negative. By the simple act of thinking positive thoughts and speaking positive words we attract positive energy.

There is tremendous power in our thoughts. What we think can make or break our soul. We can choose to strengthen the soul through positive and healing thoughts or kill it through negative thoughts. It is the soul that has the power to control the mind and mind controls the body. So you see, how important it is for us to strengthen the soul. Our souls heal our body – positive self-talk begins the healing process. We can heal ourselves physically, mentally and spiritually only if we release positive energies around us. We can recharge our spirit through positive thoughts and emotions.

It is important to accept all experience as potentially good. I could forgive my enemies, even love them and thereby nullify any bad influence they may have had on me. All experiences can be positive. All are learning experiences. We are here to learn, to experiment, and to make mistakes. We need not judge ourselves harshly nor worry about other people's judgement of us.

THE POWER OF POSITIVE THINKING

It is said that you can change your life through the power of positive thinking. Terminal cancer patients have sometimes recovered through this power. When the doctors give up, it is this power that takes up its place. Why else do you think the doctors stress on the cooperation of the patient in healing? Beyond a certain point medicines have no effect, but the mind has. It transcends beyond all limits and boundaries and brings about a healing, which has not yet been explained by science.

No one really understands how or why a positive attitude helps people recover faster from surgery or cope better with serious diseases such as cancer, heart disease and AIDS. But mounting evidence suggests that these effects may have something to do with the mind's power over the immune system. Some researchers think that pessimism may stress you out too, boosting levels of destructive stress hormones in your bloodstream. Of course, it's also possible that having a positive attitude towards life makes you more likely to take better care of yourself. And you're more likely to attract people into your life – which by itself may boost your health.

What Gives Rise to Negative Emotions

To work on the positive side, one has to first know the causes that give rise to negative emotions. Here are some very common reasons that breed negativity in peoples' minds.

- Excessive expectations of what 'should' happen
- Clinging on to one negative incident and expecting it to happen all the time
- Magnifying your own problems and minimising others
- Criticising, labelling the person instead of the mistake
- All-or-nothing thinking. Classifying people into 'good' or 'bad'
- Emotional reasoning. Exaggerating thinking about the negative consequences of small incidents
- Jumping to wrong conclusions
- Building a mental filter which harps on one negative incident and ignores the ten positive incidents that take place
- Blaming yourself for others' mistakes
- Disqualifying the positive. Where bad things count, good things don't.

Get Positive

I am not saying that you should deny life's darker side or interpret every calamity as a blessing. But when calamity does strike, try not to give in to despair or fatalism. Concluding that you personally have been singled out for suffering, refusing to see any silver lining and abandoning all hope may not only be a recipe for illness: Such attitudes are also not a great way to go through life. Try to recognise that your grief and pain, however real and deep, are only part of a larger picture – and that this picture includes many elements of pleasure, success and meaning.

Sometimes sufferings bring about a different perspective of life. I once spent a few days in the hospital when I broke my arm. I found that some women exhibited an amazing sense of optimism. Some of them had been operated for cancer and had lost a limb, but they had managed to overcome the obsession with their bodies. As a result, they discovered other interests and talents, such as literature, painting or music.

Remember that even if you can't change the circumstances of your life, you can change your attitude! Just the feeling that you have some say in your own life seems to be good for you – both emotionally and physically. People who don't believe that they have any control over their lives develop a sense of passivity and helplessness – and this sense has been linked to poor health in the same way that feeling loved and hopeful have been linked to better health.

Express Negative Emotions

Just as a termite eats silently into the core of wood, reducing it to worthless powder, negative emotions reduce the human soul into worthless sawdust. They eat into the psyche, ravaging the health and happiness of the person. Why should one want to cling on to negative emotions like anger, frustration, fear or disgust?

At the same time, there is no need for anyone to feel ashamed about the negative emotions that arise in the mind, from time to time. We are neither super humans nor saints. We are normal human beings who are likely to suffer from various kinds of emotions, some good, some bad, at all times. The trick is not to succumb to the negative emotions but gain control over them. To do so, one must understand the power of positive thinking and positive emotions. An unhappy person sees only misery all around him while a happy person can only detect happiness all around.

Negativity or negative emotions do nothing but harm to the mind and body. Agreed that it is not an easy task to control one's emotions nor does it happen in a matter of days, but it is a process that can bring joy in our lives, for ever.

For our own well-being and good health, we need to get rid of the negative emotions that cloud our minds. Suppressing emotional expression can be harmful because these processes require energy, impeding our coping ability, impairing our immune functioning.

Expressing the emotions is better than repressing them, because it allows a flow of truthfulness in the body and spirit. If emotions are very strong, however, expressing them can create both external and internal tumult. The external turmoil occurs when we pour our strong emotions all over some unfortunate soul and try to make him or her responsible for our mood. The internal confusion occurs when we realise we have startled or hurt someone with our outpouring, which makes us feel dismayed and ashamed of ourselves. Then we either repress the emotions again, or express them even more loudly, neither of which will help anyone.

When we express our emotions, we hand them over to the outside world, where we hope they will be noticed, honoured, healed and transformed into something bright and beautiful. Emotional repression, on the other hand, makes us dependent on the body or the subconscious, mind that can only hold so much repressed material before it has to get rid of something. When you hand over your emotional responsibilities to your body, it stores them somewhere until they eventually show up as pain or illness. If you order your subconscious 'No anger or grief, okay?' your unconscious works very hard to obey you, but it has to create something else with all your pent-up anger and grief. So what does it do? It expresses those emotions in some other manner. It represses them and allows them to be manifested as severe bodily pains or mental traumas.

The repression of emotion has serious drawbacks. On the other hand, when you listen to, honour and channel your emotions, you don't need to hand them off to anyone or anything. Emotional channelling lets you handle your emotions all by yourself. When you are able to take care of your own emotions, they will take care of you in ways you may not be able to believe right now.

All emotions are messages from our subconscious aspects to our conscious ones. Emotions may spring from our bodies, from our deep memories, or from unused and unnoticed aspects of our psyche. Strong or uncontrollable emotions carry not just truth but enormous amounts of energy. Strong emotions are the energey warehouse of the soul.

All emotions are tools for our use, if we accept them, channel them responsibly and take the time to listen to their healing messages. Emotional channelling reminds us that a healthy psyche is a complete one. Completeness includes light and dark, good and bad, love and hate, perfection and flaws, solemnity and silliness, wisdom and idiocy, and everything else. If you ignore your own shadowy emotions and try to hide them, or throw them out with the trash, they may loom up and attack you with your own repressed energy. Emotional channelling does not interfere with the expression of our needs, feelings and moods to the aware and supportive people in our lives. Rather, it offers a stronger and more personally empowering support.

In order to remain normal and human from this moment onwards, you'll need an environment that lets you cry when you're sad, squeal and jump when you're exhilarated, move quickly when you're anxious, protect yourself when you're fearful, stomp and snap when you're angry, dance when you're happy, and grieve when you lose someone or something. Confident people accept and honour all human emotions.

RECAP

- Most of us learn to relax physically but mental relaxation remains far from being achieved.
- The whole purpose of physical relaxation is to allow yourself to recharge your emotional and mental batteries.
- There is tremendous power in our thoughts. Our limitations and joys begin in our hearts.
- Emotions play a major role in our health and happiness. Emotions may spring from our bodies, from our deep memories, or from unused and unnoticed aspects of our psyches.
- All emotions are tools for our use, if we accept them, channel them responsibly, and take the time to listen to their healing messages.
- Positive emotions give you energy, while negative emotions deplete your energy.
- Emotional energy is a far more refined form of energy, and it is absolutely essential to healthy emotional functioning.
- The more we learn about the mind–body connection, the more we realise the benefits of having a control over our emotions.

A CALM STATE OF MIND

The mind is like a still lake. When ripples of worry are cast on it, the waves arise and the surface is disturbed. Physical relaxation is comparatively easier to achieve. It opens the way to the higher states of mental and metaphysical relaxation. Those who can enter a high state of mental relaxation at will find that physical relaxation comes automatically.

Stress is the byword of the modern era. We all need stress in our lives in perfect balance with all other factors of life today. Stress keeps us alert, on our toes, ready for action, and helps us achieve our best performance. One only has to see trained athletes on the starting blocks tensing, steeling and honing every nerve and muscle in their body, preparing for that instant action that will make up valuable seconds. Competitors on TV quiz games use that state of tension to ensure focus of concentration and alertness. Stress helps us win, stress helps us concentrate; balanced stress ensures a good performance.

It is all a question of balance between stress and calm, for stress cannot exist where calm is total. Alternate ripples of stress and calm create harmony, create balance, but if the ripples become waves, calm ceases to exist. Once the waves become tumultuous, they can threaten to shake a body apart. The height of the storm is scary, it is impossible to think clearly or see beyond the incoming waves, to hear above the roar of uncertainty. Gradually, all around become affected and in turn become stressful, others reflect the turmoil, and a vicious circle is created. Patience thins, tempers flare and the all-consuming vortex is born. The alternative is to swallow the anger, internalising it and filing it away until the drawer becomes too full and bursts open or the anger turns inwards and becomes depression. Both emotions can eat away at the body and its energy, becoming physical ailments as the subconscious cries out for help.

Calm is the oil that spreads on troubled waters, for calm overrides stress, and once inner calm is established, the rampaging tiger becomes as friendly as a domestic cat. For stress can become a friend once calm is established. Yet how can this process begin to re-establish in the chaos of the modern world?

A Technique for Inducing Relaxation

- Choose a room where you can find three elements – silence, solitude and stillness.
- Sit in a comfortable position on the floor and take three deep breaths.
- Close the eyes and expel the breath. Switch off the attention and the energy from your senses.
- Now, direct your attention inward and sense the heartbeat. Concentrate on the rhythm of the beats till your mind is totally lulled.
- Relinquish all your thoughts and enter a passive, unconscious state of mental blankness.
- Your aim should be to enter this state of blankness or the 'No Mind' state of Zen.
- After entering the zone of silence and mindlessness, still the thoughts for several minutes.
- Now think of some happy incident in your life, something that brought immense joy to you and dwell on it. Visualise it. Mentally go through the same pleasant experience over and over again until you forget all worries entirely.
- Sit quietly and meditate over the joy of the experience. Smile as your heart opens up joyfully.

At the end of the exercise, you will find yourself rejuvenated and joyful. The sense of happiness will carry itself through the day.

Autogenic Training and Self-Hypnosis

Autogenic, one of the most powerful therapies as far as mind training is concerned, means 'self-regulation or self-generation'. It refers to the way in which your mind can influence your body to balance the self-regulative systems that control circulation, breathing, heart rate, and so on.

Autogenic training allows you to control stress by training your autonomic nervous system to become relaxed. This wonderful technique can produce a blissful feeling of warmth and heaviness in every part of the body and induce spectacular healing in sick and diseased bodies.

It helps if you learn progressive relaxation first. Autogenic training will then teach you to respond, in a passive manner, to verbal and visual cues that reduce tension. By focusing on relaxing phrases and images, the training conditions positive, relaxing responses, such as rhythmic breathing and heart rate.

Autogenic training is based on the notion of passive concentration: that is, you try to achieve your goal of relaxation by not working actively to do so. Choose times and places that are feasible for an uninterrupted session. Wear comfortable clothes. Sit in a position that allows total support for your entire body. When you begin autogenic training, first work on reducing your heart rate and calming your breathing; then you can move on to trying to evoke warm, heavy, relaxed sensations in your limbs and body.

As you practice, try to combine phrases with images in order to keep your mind occupied. If thoughts do intrude into your session, just observe them and let them go.

How to Do It

Here is an example of a session using the right phrases and images. You can run through this mentally as you practise, or you can make a tape recording to guide you through the session.

- Sit comfortably and gently roll your head in a half circle in front of you. Roll from side to side a few times then bring your head up to face forward.
- Take a deep breath in, drawing the air deep into your stomach. Slowly release the breath.

- Concentrate on your breathing, which is smooth and rhythmic. Imagine that your breaths are like waves lapping at the shore.
- Keep this image in your mind as you repeat to yourself, 'My breathing is rhythmic and smooth... my breathing is rhythmic and smooth.'
- With each breath, feel relaxation wash over you like the waves. The waves wash over your feet and legs, your stomach and chest. Feel them cover your arms, your neck, and your head. Your arms and legs feel warm and heavy.
- Experience the waves of relaxation sweep over you. Feel your limbs growing heavier, warmer. Your breathing is calm, rhythmic and smooth.
- Now move your focus to your heart. Imagine the waves of relaxation washing over you, calming your breathing and your heart.
- Repeat to yourself, 'My heartbeat is gentle and even... My heartbeat is gentle and even.' 'I feel quiet, calm, relaxed... My heartbeat is gentle and even.'
- Your body feels peaceful and tranquil, you are relaxed. Concentrate now on your right arm and hand. Tell yourself, 'My right arm and hand feel warm and heavy... My right arm and hand feel warm and heavy.'
- Imagine the sun shining on your arm and hand. Feel the warmth spread through your arm and hand as they grow heavier and heavier. Say to yourself, 'My right arm and hand feel warm and heavy...'
- Now focus on your left arm and hand. Say to yourself, 'My left arm and hand feel warm and heavy... My left arm and hand feel warm and heavy.'

- ❄ Again imagine the sun shining on your arm and hand, or that they are soaking in a hot tub. Feel the warmth spread through your arm and hand, and feel them grow heavier. Say to yourself, 'My left arm and hand feel warm and heavy...'
- ❄ Concentrate now on both of your arms and hands. They both feel warm and heavy. Say to yourself, 'Both of my arms and hands are warm and heavy... My right arm and left arm are warm and heavy...' Feel the warmth flow through your arms and hands, down into your fingers to the tips. You feel relaxed all over as your arms and hands get warmer and heavier.
- ❄ While your arms are warm and heavy, scan your body from head to toe to find any muscle tension in other parts of your body. Make sure your shoulders are dropped and relaxed, your jaw is not clenched, your legs are relaxed. You should feel relaxed all over, your mind free from thought.
- ❄ Now turn your concentration to your legs. Feel the warmth and heaviness from your arms flow down into your legs. Say to yourself, 'My legs and feet are warm and heavy... My legs and feet are warm and heavy.'
- ❄ Imagine bathing in the sun and feel the warmth spread over your body, radiating through your arms and hands, down through your legs and feet. Say to yourself, 'My feet and hands are warm and heavy... My arms and legs are warm and heavy.' All of your limbs now feel warm and heavy.
- ❄ Your body is relaxed and calm; your breathing is deep and rhythmic; your heart is beating gently and evenly.
- ❄ To complete the autogenic exercise, take a deep breath and exhale.

- Picture yourself now in the room where you began the session. You are calm and relaxed, and you will become more relaxed each time you do this exercise.
- Take a few more deep breaths, open your eyes, and you will feel relaxed yet alert and refreshed.

After the Session

If you are going to resume physical activity, you can follow your autogenic exercises with stretching to stimulate your muscles. If you find yourself yawning, don't assume that you are now tired. Take this as a sign that the exercise has worked - that you are relaxed and free from tension.

A Word of Warning

While autogenic training is effective in reducing stress, tension and anxiety, it is not recommended for people with severe mental disorders. You should have a complete physical examination before beginning to practise autogenic training, and people with diabetes, hypoglycaemia, heart conditions, and high or low blood pressure should practise only under the supervision of their physician. If you feel any adverse side effects, discontinue your practice and consult an experienced autogenic training instructor.

Self-Hypnosis and Auto-Suggestion

Hypnosis, auto-suggestion and autogenic training - all these are allied therapies to bring relaxation to the mind. They are similar to the extent that the power of suggestion is the primary element that works in each of them. You might have watched shows where mass hypnotism is performed by magicians and hypnotists but self-hypnosis can also be performed with great effectiveness.

Hypnosis is merely a state of mind in which you are very relaxed. You are paying complete attention to the suggestions you want to implant. You do not criticise the suggestions made, and accept them at face value. Self-hypnosis is used to directly program your unconscious mind with affirmations and suggestions that would otherwise have to run through critical processes in your mind. You can use this programming as an effective method to reduce stress and induce relaxation.

Normal hypnosis is often ineffective in stress reduction, as it requires the presence of a hypnotist. Self-hypnosis, however, is just as easy and has the additional benefit that you can completely control the inputs to your mind when you are in a suggestible state.

Hypnotising Yourself

- The first few times that you use self-hypnosis, it is best to find a place where you can be undisturbed for a while. Sit or lie down, eliminate any distractions and relax. This puts you in the best possible conditions for using the technique. However, as you get more practice, you will find that you can use self-hypnosis almost anywhere. Obviously, it should not be used when you need to be alert – e.g. when driving or operating machinery, etc.
- The first step is to relax yourself: close your eyes, and try using imagery of waves of relaxation running down your body from your scalp downwards, washing out stress. Let the waves run in time with your breathing, first washing down over your head, then your neck, then your torso, then arms, and finally your legs. Feel the muscles in your body relaxing as the waves of relaxation wash over them.
- Alternative techniques can involve fixing your eyes on a spot on the wall, or riding down in a lift/elevator from the top of a tall building, slowly dropping down into relaxation and drowsiness. The method you choose to induce hypnosis is up to you.

- The next step is to use suggestion to deepen the state. This is as simple as saying to yourself some thing like 'I am feeling relaxed and comfortable. With every breath I am becoming more relaxed and more comfortable.'
- Once you are completely relaxed and focused on your own suggestions, you are in a useful state of self-hypnosis. One suggestion you can usefully embed is that when you repeat a particular trigger word to yourself you will relax into this state.

It would be worthwhile to decide the suggestions that you want to apply in the hypnotic state.

Suggestions can be simple affirmations that can alter the damage done by negative thinking. You can also use suggestions to make psychological changes or reinforce confidence to help to achieve goals that you have set.

Once you have decided what you want to use in suggestions, spend a little time working out a form of words for each suggestion that is short, positive and powerful. Repeat these suggestions to yourself when you have reached a self-hypnotic state.

Effective use of suggestion can build confidence, reinforce goals by etching them into your mind. It can reduce stress and motivate and energise the mind when you are feeling sluggish.

Recap

- Physical relaxation is comparatively easier to achieve. It opens the way to the higher states of mental and metaphysical relaxation.
- Those who can enter a high state of mental relaxation at will find that physical relaxation comes automatically.
- Autogenic training allows you to control stress by

training your autonomic nervous system to become relaxed.

- Self-hypnotism can be used as an effective method to reduce stress and induce relaxation.
- Rational thinking is one of the most successful techniques to combat negative thinking.

CHAPTER FOUR

Spiritual Relaxation

The spirit is an amalgam of the mind, soul and emotions. Man's nature is a blend of three elements – physical, mental and spiritual. The harmonious development of any one of these factors depends upon the state of the other two. On a higher plane of life, there is emotional well-being, a sense of peace and a positive outlook. The natural outcome of these elements is a well-balanced life, which is in harmony with nature and everything around us. When one is in harmony with nature, it leads to happiness and contentment. With happiness and contentment comes the total health package consisting of a healthy mind, body and soul. The strength of our body doesn't come from muscles alone, it comes from the mind, which is the most powerful element of human life. And this power that comes from within is not solely dependent on food or exercise alone.

The millions of tiny cells that form each and every part of our body are created and kept energised by thoughts and biological forces. It is your mind that controls all activities; the body can do nothing without the consent of the brain. Most people concentrate only upon food, air and exercise to keep their bodies healthy, but a time comes when health fails despite the best of food and exercise regimen. Then comes the realisation that the battery of physical body needs to be recharged with spiritual enlightenment. Food alone doesn't support life. If it did, one could put food in the body of a dead man, pump some oxygen into his lungs through the lung machine and he would come alive. But it doesn't happen so, does it?

We can never achieve lasting happiness till we learn to seek spiritual attainment. Even if we attain the perfect material conditions of which we dream, happiness wouldn't come unless we can attain spiritual satisfaction. Spirituality brings an inner joy to our lives.

You are your own greatest enemy and you are your own greatest friend
If you are the enemy of your soul, your soul will act as your enemy
If you are your soul's friend, your soul will be your friend.

—Bhagavad Gita

Spirituality has nothing to do with religion. A lot many people confuse themselves with the misinterpretation that the two are synonymous. Spirituality does not need any rituals other than those required for developing the self-realisation and self-actualisation goals. It merely relates to an upliftment of the mind and soul. When the mind is rid of the negative thoughts and can travel to the higher realms of refined ones, it has begun its journey towards spirituality.

As Sri Sri Ravi Shankar says, 'Religion is the banana skin and spirituality is the banana. The misery in the world is because we throw away the banana and we are holding on to the dry skin. So, we need to enhance the spiritual aspect of our life.'

You can change your world. I am not referring to the world that exists all around us but the one that is within each of us. If we all make an earnest effort to change that world, the external world will eventually become a better place. The problem is that we all try to change everything around us but neglect to alter anything that is wrong with us. Ask anyone, and he will tell you a hundred things that are wrong around him; but ask him if everything is alright within his own self, and he will not know the answer.

The solution lies in clearing up the garbage that lies within our own soul before we take a big broom and try cleaning up the society. What is the society? It is you and I; we make the society. So, how can we improve the society if we continue to be rotten inside? And believe me, we need to change not for others but for our own happiness. Cleaning up the garbage within will bring us true happiness and joy. We blame everyone and everything around us, talk of corruption and violence and of everything that is wrong with the world, but we forget that it is our contribution to the world that makes all the difference.

Tranquillity, harmony, quietness, these are words that find way into all our wishes. We all want them. What does inner peace really mean? Can we buy it? Can we learn to acquire it? Does it really exist? Almost everyone muses over these questions at some time in life. Most of us consciously experience different stages in life where inner peace is more strongly experienced. People rush from one spiritual teacher to another, change from one religion to another, enlist themselves for various spiritual courses and practise all kinds of techniques to find some peace.

It seems that everyone, either consciously or subconsciously, directly or indirectly, is seeking this elusive goal. What is it? Inner peace is that state of being where the mind ceases to look outward, where it stops searching for things outside of itself and is content by itself. No longer does it require external factors to bring a sense of joy and happiness to it.

The mind, body and spirit are intrinsically woven with each other. Psycho-neuro-immunology, the mind–body healing, professes that you cannot be healed until all the three components are in equilibrium.

How can the mind find the inner peace when it is filled with fear, anxiety or worry?

Instead of carrying their weight as a burden, you have to assure yourself that serenity is your natural state, and take appropriate action to remove whatever is blocking that inner peace. Perhaps you stop to say a prayer, repeat an empowering affirmation. Maybe you forgive someone or act with compassion for another. Try to remember the many mountains you have climbed in the past, or take an objective look at your current state and rate it on a scale of 1–10. Maybe you ask for help or guidance, or simply surrender your worry to the universe. Whatever path you take, it is with the belief that serenity can be yours... right now... in this place. You just have to decide to take a break, shift gears and stop the stress that is like a drape over your natural serene state. It is chronic daily stress that wears down our courage, faith and optimism. Taking daily 'uplifting' breaks builds our resilience and keeps us connected to our core of inner peace.

On days when you feel a bit hollow inside, uninspired, perhaps wondering if this is all there is to life, don't throw up your hands, saying, 'Some day, when I retire and have more time, I'm going to do what I've been meaning to do.' Instead, stop and offer a prayer of healing for someone in pain, write a note of thanks, or call someone to let them know they are loved. You might register for a cause you wish to support, or teach someone something you've learned. If you decide to act in meaningful ways on a daily basis, regardless of how small the steps might be – you begin walking on the path of serenity.

It is amazing what a small move in thinking can do to make peace a reality in our daily lives. Our thoughts change our expectations. Our expectations change our decisions. Our decisions change our behaviours. Our behaviours change our experience. And, of course, our experience changes our thoughts. Serenity is not to be found, but simply allowed to grow. We do not need 'to get away' to experience serenity, we need to 'make it our way'.

Ultimately, inner peace is a function of one's own consciousness and is completely independent of all external input. Because of the nature of the universe, real inner peace can never be permanently found in the external world. Nature is composed of a natural rhythm and cycle. Night follows day. Cold follows heat. Pain follows pleasure. Similarly, the upswing in life is almost always followed by a downswing; it is only the length and span of each experience that may alter. For instance, sometimes the happy phase is longer than the sorrowful one, and at other times, it is the reverse. To accept this phenomenon one must train the mind to remember that nothing lasts for ever and all that goes up will come down at some point or the other.

Detoxifying the Soul

Soul is the combined product of mental and emotional energies. A peaceful soul can change the way you perceive things. It can keep us in the highest, most productive, happiest and healthiest mental and emotional state even in the worst of the physical conditions. An enriched soul can bring a lasting sense of peace and joy to a person. A joyful soul can bring about a blissful existence, and if a person is joyful, can good health be far behind?

Over the years we spend on this planet, our souls get jaded and corrupted with the many negative thoughts we harbour in our minds and the materialistic approach we begin to take in our life. This makes it impossible for us to find peace and happiness, or for that matter, relaxation. Toxic thoughts, toxic feelings and emotions prey on the soul causing enough restlessness in us to make us unhealthy.

Why do some of us find it difficult to sleep or relax? If the causes were traced, most of them would lead to toxic thoughts. Guilt about wrongdoings, remorse, regret, jealousy and frustration – these are some of the common factors that leave people sleepless and restless. During the daytime it is easy to escape the inner voice, busy as we are in our work; come night, and we begin to be hounded by the inner voice. There is no escape from its condemnation for the wrong acts carried out during the day. It fatigues the mind, and we wake up feeling as exhausted as when we went to bed, because there has been no respite for the mind and the soul.

The toxic emotions need to be cleansed and the soul has to be detoxified before we begin to contemplate a relaxed life.

Healing the Soul

What is soul healing? Soul healing is the exploration and application of the true radiant nature of the soul. Soul healing allows one to heal and transcend one's self from the ego to the core of being the Self. In essence, soul healing is a transformation and spiritual journey of the ego en route to the greater, or higher Self.

In essence, soul healing is a process where you 'become' love. Soul healing allows one to accept full responsibility for his/her own motives, intentions, emotions, desires, thoughts, behaviours and actions. By combining physical, emotional, mental and spiritual realms, soul healing enables persons to discover their collective consciousness and bring forth harmony.

Soul healing unlocks barriers that have essentially held a person back. Soul healing helps you to discover past lives, personal essence and energetically clears chakras and meridian points. Soul healing also helps discover the symbols that unlock past information; it makes one aware of one's mission and purpose in life. Soul healing can release energetic patterns from past traumas, karmic attachments, interconnection with God and much more.

When our bodies become poisoned, whether from alcohol or drugs or environmental toxins, we must go through a detoxification process to regain health. Similarly, when the soul has suffered from the poisonous ill effects of our thoughts, it needs to be healed and detoxified too.

Just as our bodies can be weakened by exposure to poisons, our minds are susceptible to the toxins of craving, aversion and ignorance. These mental toxins arise naturally in human life, and unfortunately, our culture often encourages them. Most of us live in a toxic soup of fear, anger, envy and impatience. Just as the addict indulges in unhealthy behaviour that, for a while, masks the nature of the poison, we delude ourselves into thinking that our unhappiness can be removed by material things and sensual pleasures. Happiness arises naturally when we become free of the mental and emotional toxins that poison us.

Meditation is a tool we can use to detoxify the mind. When we meditate, we suspend our indulgence in toxic thoughts. When we open the mind and just observe, we can begin to see the source of our difficulties.

When we quieten the mind, we can see the source of our misery in our toxic memories and thoughts. We may find that sitting still stimulates the flow of negative thoughts and emotions. Just as an alcoholic in detox may experience shakiness, hallucinations and unpleasant body sensations, when we attempt to still the mind, the mental impurities may manifest themselves. This is the opportunity to go beyond our addiction to them and observe them at their source. The sources of misery are not outside us. They are within the structure of the body/mind. In the peace of a quieter mind we can see the truth.

RECAP

- Man's nature is a blend of three elements – physical, mental and spiritual. The harmonious development of any one of these factors depends upon the state of the other two factors.
- Spirituality has nothing to do with religion. It merely relates to an upliftment of the mind and soul.
- Inner peace is that state of being where the mind ceases to look outward, where it stops searching for things outside of itself and is content by itself.

- Inner peace is a function of one's own consciousness and is completely independent of all external input.
- Soul is the combined product of mental and emotional energies. A peaceful soul can change the way you perceive things.
- It can keep us in the highest, most productive, happiest and healthiest mental and emotional state even in the worst of the physical conditions.
- Just as our bodies can be weakened by exposure to poisons, our minds are susceptible to the toxins of craving, aversion and ignorance.
- Happiness arises naturally when we become free of the mental and emotional toxins that poison us.

MEDITATION

The word 'meditation' means different things to different people. There are hundreds of different schools of mediation, many associated with some form of religious practice and many that are not. Some of these varied forms of meditation may include techniques such as complex visualisation or chanting words or sounds known as 'mantras'. Meditation is a truly holistic activity in that, ideally, the whole system of body, mind and spirit is involved and benefited. It is one of the greatest methods to unwind, relax the mind and trigger the body's own natural relaxation response. Meditation is nothing but the concentration of all mental energies into a single direction.

It is the practice of concentrating on an object, word, or idea to clear the mind, relax the body, and achieve a state of heightened awareness and enlightenment. Meditation has been a feature of many religions, but it can also serve as a practical, calming therapy. It cuts off the sensory input, halts the demands of the brain and gives the mind a chance to rest. Research projects have shown that meditation can lower blood pressure, reduce the body's metabolic rate and ameliorate many stress-related disorders.

Physical Benefits

The physical benefits of mediation include relaxation, improvement of sleeping patterns, lowering of high blood pressure, recovery from fatigue and general beneficial effect on most stress-related diseases. Meditation slows down the rate of breathing, helps the muscles relax, gives the body time to eliminate lactic acid and other waste products, reduces anxiety and reduces stress headaches.

Awareness of the body is an essential part of effective meditation. Many of the emotional stresses and upsets that people experience can be held as tensions in the body and therefore be fairly unconscious. Through the process of conscious relaxation of body and breathing that meditation entails, these stresses can be unlocked from their hiding places in the muscles and joints and simultaneously released.

Meditation fortifies the immune system and promotes physical health. The Alpha and Theta brainwaves that occur during the process lower the blood pressure and the pulse rate. It is an excellent remedy for insomnia and other stress-related ailments. With the meditative state of mind come the factors like self-healing of the mind as well as the body.

Mental Benefits

Meditation teaches one to fix his mind more firmly in the present reality, to have accurate and easy recall to lead a more wholesome, happy, healthy and meaningful life. It eliminates stressful thoughts and promotes clear thinking. It also helps sharpen focus and concentration. It also reduces irritability.

Meditation can improve the ability to concentrate, the ability to listen, both to others and yourself. Although people cannot change their external conditions to any large extent, they can take the responsibility of changing their attitudes and reactions, the way the mind interacts with the world. One of the most effective and safest ways to bring about this change is to meditate.

The path of meditation offers a way of becoming more awake and alive to every aspect, inner and outer. The practice known as 'mindfulness' is simply carrying this present-centred attention into one's daily life and activities, whether walking or running or doing household chores.

Spiritual Benefits

With meditation, a whole new realm is unravelled to the mind. It promotes a spiritualistic thinking, which brings inner peace to an individual and raises the individual towards the higher realm of celestial vibrations.

Meditation is very useful if:

- You have been under long-term stress
- You have been under short-term stress which has caused adrenaline to be released into your bloodstream
- You have been worrying about problems
- You have been physically active

The Posture, Place and Practice

How often should I practice? How should I sit? These are the questions often asked by those starting out on the path of meditation. For both these questions there are no 'right' answers, no one 'proper' way of meditating. Individuals explore for themselves, evolving an effective and appropriate practice. As for time and frequency, some schools suggests many hours a day, some advocate quality rather than quantity, a short focused period of meditation of five or ten minutes.

Each individual has his own parameters and should follow them. Comfort should be one of the prime criteria while meditating. You can't meditate if you are sitting on thorns unless you are a yogi. Similarly, you should meditate only for as much time as you can control your mind. Begin with a couple of minutes and work up to longer time, which is more logical than forcing yourself to sit while fidgeting or watching the clock just because you have been told that you should meditate for a specific number of minutes.

There is no compromise on the posture, though. Meditation seems to work best when the spine is straight, but relaxed and vertical. There are several reasons for this. First, sitting upright is a very good way of staying awake and alert while the eyes are closed and the attention drawn inwards. If the body is upright, the breath can begin to move in and out freely and without obstruction. Also the muscles of the torso and spine have a chance to unclog themselves of old tensions.

Sitting upright sends a message to the unconscious that although your eyes are closed you are not going to sleep, as you would when lying down. On a more subtle level, the body's Qi energy, or life force, is able to move more freely if the spine is straight. Energy cannot move through tense muscles, so a relaxed way of sitting needs to be found.

If you find it difficult to sit on the floor, sitting in a chair is also acceptable. If sitting cross-legged on the floor, you will probably find it helpful to have a firm cushion at least 2–3 inches thick, under your bottom. This lifts the spine so that it is easier to sit upright. You may choose to kneel, in which case, sitting on a larger cushion or a meditation bench would be advisable to prevent cutting off circulation to the legs. If you feel most comfortable sitting in a chair, choose one that is the right height for you. A firm, straight-backed chair is better than an armchair, and if you can sit up unsupported, it is still better.

As for place, it is best to opt for one that is absolutely bereft of noise and disturbance. It is easier to meditate when the room is cool and slightly dark rather than a sunny one, especially in our country where heat makes it impossible to do anything except think about the temperature.

Focusing

Your breath also provides an ever-present and easily accessible focus for concentration. One is always breathing! Many schools of meditation, like Vipassana, teach how to focus on the breath in various ways.

This may involve imagining that the breath originates in one particular point of the body. The points most usually focused on are the hara or tan tien – just below and behind the navel, or the heart, in the centre of the chest. The crown of the head, the base of the spine or the soles of the feet may all be included in the awareness. Focusing on the breath can also take the form of noticing the physical changes as the breath moves in and out, either at the nostrils or the abdomen. Meditation can be as simple as this, just breathing while sitting.

You can meditate anytime and anywhere if you learn the art of mindfulness. Mindfulness is a Zen meditation technique in which full focus is given to the present. Make a conscious effort to practise it. If you are chopping vegetables, empty your mind of everything else: focus on the act of chopping, the colours of the foods, their aromas. Love the sensation of being fully engaged with the world around you. This practice invariably leads to efficiency and relaxation of the mind. The essence is to 'be there' and 'with it' a hundred per cent, no matter what you are doing.

A Simple Form of Meditating

Sit upright with erect spine and closed or downcast eyes. Concentrate on your respiration. Notice your inhalation and your exhalation. Observe the fine points that are involved in the process. Don't try to change your breathing. Just watch the breath flow in and out, in a passive manner.

As you observe your breath, memories, thoughts and feelings may arise. Become aware of them, but don't cling to them. Don't try to make them go away. Just observe them dispassionately and let them go. Continue to follow your breath and stay awake and aware.

As thoughts and emotions arise, observe how they arise. How do they come to you? As discomfort arises, observe how it arises. What is the source of the discomfort?

Use this quiet time to learn about yourself. Allow the impurities of mind to arise and dissipate. Be patient. Sit in the light of true self-healing and experience the truth beyond mind and matter.

Meditation with Imagery

When meditation is combined with imagery, it can bring about total rejuvenating experience. All you have to do is to create a mental image of a pleasant and relaxing place in your mind. Involve all your senses in the imagery: see the place, hear the sounds, smell the aromas, feel the temperature and the movement of the wind. Enjoy the location in your mind.

In all cases, it is important to keep your attention focused. If external thoughts or distractions wander in, let them drift out. If necessary, visualise attaching the thoughts to objects and then move the objects out of your attention.

Some time back, while travelling in the train, I came across a Korean master who was teaching a new concept in meditation, called smile meditation. We spoke about this therapy in great details. He told me that smile meditation advocates using the inner smile for calming the mind. The next time you notice yourself feeling tense or stressed, try the technique of the 'inner smile'. In ancient Chinese medicine a similar approach to this is said to activate the tan tein, the energy store of your body, just below our navel. Laughter therapy is based on the same principle and the effectiveness of a good belly laugh is also dependent on the activation of the tan tein.

After I returned from the trip, I decided to try out the technique of inner smile and was pleasantly surprised to note that it worked very well, indeed. Think of something that makes you feel happy: this could be the smell of freshly-baked bread or a joyful moment from your past – anything that brings a smile in your heart. Allow this smile to travel within you until it sits in your abdomen radiating warmth throughout the body. A refreshing feeling of lightness and happiness covers the mind after you have enjoyed the inner smile. It actually keeps you happy and smiling through the day.

Smile Meditation

Smile meditation is based on Taoist meditation practice. In this kind of meditation, we have to use the smile that we give others for our own good. The inner smile is an opportunity to offer a smile to oneself. It can be done in a seated meditation session or in the midst of daily life.

- To begin, find a comfortable posture for meditation (seated on a cushion or blanket, in a chair, or against a wall). It may be helpful to set a timer to 10, 20 or 30 minutes so you can sink deeply into your meditation without wondering about the time.
- Place your hands on your knees in Dhyana Mudra (index and thumb touching), with palms facing up to open your awareness or palms facing down to calm the mind. Do a body scan and relax any tension you may be holding. Let your spine rise from the root of the pelvis. Draw your chin slightly down and lengthen the back of your neck.
- Begin by generating a feeling of natural happiness as if it emanates from the backs of the eyes. If the feeling does not come naturally, remind yourself of any experience of natural joy – for example, the face of a joyous child. You can use any past experience of happiness to light up your face and bring a smile.

- Once you generate the feeling of this smile, let it radiate down the backs of your eyes like a waterfall. Visualise this meditative stream flowing down the centre of your spine, to your heart and lungs, then into your stomach and spleen (under your left lower ribs), and liver (under your right lower ribs). Let it run down through the kidneys (back ribs), the colon and intestines (belly), down into your genitals, and out into your legs and feet.
- You can repeat the sweep from the backs of the eyes to the feet or do one long, slow sweep. The inner smile can be its own complete meditation or it may lead you into an effortless meditative absorption.
- Remain in this happy position for as long as you wish. When you have finished, bring your hands together and complete your meditation with a moment of gratitude, reflection or prayer to seal the energy of your meditation into your life. Remember that you can cultivate the inner smile anytime throughout the day to fill the heart with compassion.

Recap

- Researchers have found scientific evidence about the holistic healing effects of meditation and prayer.
- Meditation promotes the Alpha and Theta brain waves that are known to be highly calming in nature.
- Meditation induces relaxation, lowers blood pressure, reduces the body's metabolic rate and ameliorates many stress-related disorders. It is one of the greatest methods to relax the mind

and trigger the body's own natural relaxation response.

- Meditation can improve the ability to concentrate and to listen.
- Meditation combined with imagery can bring about total rejuvenating experience.

Relaxation and Spirituality

Why do people turn spiritual with age? This is question I had often asked myself during my youth. Why don't we feel so spiritual when we are young?

I guess we are so wrapped up in the business of living that we forget that there are some things beyond the materialistic. Then comes a day when the materialistic things do not bring peace to our soul and we begin to feel the need for something else. We realise that we are missing out on the more important things in life. There is restlessness and a feeling of discontent. This is the time we often switch on to the spiritual aspects, and spiritualism becomes a way of life. Of course, there are many young people who are as spiritual as the old ones or vice versa. It is all a matter of awakening and realisation.

Spirituality is the science that teaches us to free and uncondition our minds. Spirituality is virtually as enriching for your life as adding the figure 1 to many zeroes. If you add one to six zeroes it multiplies to become a million. And without the one, the zeroes have no identity at all.

Spirituality promotes a relaxed state of mind. It brings serenity, inner peace and placidity in our lives. Getting spiritual also means bowing out of the rat race and accepting the higher goals in life. It means leaving behind the negative thoughts and emotions and switching to the higher plane of universal good.

The way to proceed on the spiritual path is to control the five vices that are the Satan's tools to put us on the destructive path. These vices come in the form of lust, anger, greed, attachment and ego.

1. Lust: Lust comes when values are gone, when we cannot see beyond the gloss and glitter of materialism, when we don't know what we want; so we want everything, whether it's right for us or not. It also comes in the form of sexual passion.

2. Anger: Anger comes when we are hollow within. It comes because we haven't been able to get what we want. It is the manifestation of our frustrations in life. It brings only misery in its wake – for us and the others around us.

3. Jealousy: This green-eyed serpent occurs when we are insecure and frustrated. Instead of directing our energies on a positive note, we begin to direct them into the negative territory. By being jealous, we exhibit our inadequacies and dissatisfaction.

4. Attachment: God sent perfect souls to the earth, but the souls developed egoistic attachment to the other actors, certain scenes and conditions in the cosmic drama of life. Attachments come because we are afraid of losing. They bring with them misery and unhappiness.

5. Ego: It is a feeling that 'I am something'. It has been built into us; it is a reaction of the mind that eventually is looked upon as a real person. The subjective consciousness or 'I-ness' adopted by the soul in connection with the body and its environmental relationships is called ego. It is the stage of body consciousness. It is ego that makes us go through a consciousness attachment to the senses. According to Swami Sivananda, 'Ego is a steel wall that separates the man from God'.

Toxic Thoughts

What Generates Toxic Thoughts

Certain characteristics generate toxic thoughts more than others. Perfectionists, control freaks, chronic worriers and doomsday predictors excel in harbouring toxic thoughts more than those who are easy-going, friendly and optimistic.

Perfectionists are a highly stressed lot. In their drive for perfection, they bulldoze through the imperfections of the world and everyone knows that the world is more imperfect than perfect. Perhaps the perfectionist realises that the imperfections will come his way but refuses to believe it. In their minds they equate imperfections with failure. The fear of failure generates a toxic pattern of thoughts.

For the control freaks it is a different ball game altogether. When we try to exercise excessive control on people and situations, we begin to take the responsibility of things beyond our control. We take the accountability for the resultant events, which are totally out of our power. The fact is that no one has any control on anything but himself or herself. The remorse and guilt felt by the control freak for situations that are beyond control generates a toxic thought process.

The chronic worrier has the ability to worry about things that may not be on the horizon for the next one century. He worries about the doomsday, the nuclear proliferation, the growing environmental hazards and impending wars. Not that it is wrong to think about these events, but the worrier excels in producing vividly-coloured images of the unforeseen events and allows them to disturb the mind. He literally takes the responsibility of worrying about things that may never happen. In his mind, phrases like 'I can never find a suitable job', 'I will never find happiness', and 'The world is doomed' find frequent incursion.

The regretter is always a step behind the worrier. He regrets and rues all the things that have passed him by. While the worrier is worried about the future events, the regretter worries and regrets the past events. Either way, the two excel in generating toxic thoughts.

Toxic thought pattern couldn't be wiped out in a day because they are a result of many years. But they can be replaced slowly and gradually by positive thought process.

Cleansing Toxic Thoughts

The mind is the most restless thing on the earth. It runs like an unbridled horse from one thought to the other before we can catch our breath and say 'stop'. You will know what I am talking about if you have ever tried to harness your mind and meditate for a few minutes. When you understand that mind governs the body, then you begin to give more power to the mind. Thoughts have to be understood and applied in the right manner, before they become effective. They come to us in crude forms. That is why people who try to handle crude thoughts without reasoning get no result and say that thoughts are not effective.

Because thoughts can't be seen and have no physical substance, many people assume they are without power and effect. However, since the beginning of recorded time, we have been cautioned and directed by astute philosophical and spiritual teachers such as Plato, Christ and Buddha that what we focus upon eventually becomes part of our existence.

This concept, once dismissed as religious or metaphysical superstition, is now being proven by such scientific disciplines as quantum physics and neurobiology.

When we understand that our mind, body and spirit are an extremely sensitive, intricately balanced, interconnected system, the need to maintain its integrity becomes obvious. Beyond eating nutritious foods and taking dietary supplements, regular attention to good mental hygiene is one of the essential building blocks of a healthy, balanced life.

Negative, angry, sad and self-defacing thoughts are toxic to your system. They are literally poisonous. These poisons activate neuro-physiological responses within the body. These, when combined with other contributory factors, lead to the manifestations of diseases such as cancer, allergies, immune deficiencies, headaches and colitis. Within the mind this toxicity can cause depression, anxiety, worry and a sense of abandonment within the spirit.

We have been conditioned to look outside of ourselves for causes of the unpleasant or negative situations in our lives. We use excuses and blame others for what we experience. However, situations, events or people do not determine our moods or feelings. You can be as happy as you allow yourself to be. No one and no situation can make you unhappy if you don't allow them to do so. The way you think or perceive a situation will direct your feelings and moods about it. How and what you think has a profound impact upon your physical, emotional and spiritual well-being.

Toxic thought patterns lead to various forms of self-destructive behaviour, including the creation and retention of regrets that burden us. Letting go of our regrets and overcoming the anger, pain and guilt they feed requires us to identify the toxic thought patterns that support them. Writing journals, spoken or written affirmations, creative visualisations, prayer, meditation, thought analysis and sharing with others are among the spiritual and psychological tools we can use to counter toxic thought patterns.

Our ability to think can be a blessing or a curse, so we can always choose to bless ourselves. Thinking is a habit, a learned response. These learned responses are imbibed right from the day we were born and are highly influences by our growing-up surroundings. These influenced continue to affect us till we die. Like any habit or behaviour, thinking patterns and tendencies can be unlearned or changed if one is motivated. It is like deciding to stop smoking. Making a conscious decision to alter your habits and thought patterns will have a direct impact on what you experience.

If you are in the habit of using phrases like 'why me', 'poor me', 'it always happens to me', 'I never get a break', or any other negative thought patterns, you need to break the habit.

Easier said than done, it takes immense self-control to work your way out of the trap. Try the following steps to detoxify your thinking and move towards good mental hygiene:

❄ **Purge the Thought:** Most of us are unable to achieve what we set out to achieve only because of the 'I can't' thoughts that cloud our vision. Opt to empower yourself. Use your visualisation ability to reaffirm the 'I can' thoughts. Henry Ford once said, 'Whether you think you can't or whether you think you can, you're right.'

❄ **Switch the Thought:** Each time you realise that you are using the negative thought, replace it with a positive one. Shake your head, tap it with the knuckles and reinforce the replacement. We have an inherent ability to pick the thoughts of our choice. Use this ability to choose your thoughts and your feelings will follow. Create a resource of positive affirmations like 'I am strong and capable' and positive images, like a superman, to replace the negative ones. When you become aware of an uncomfortable feeling or thought, intercept it with the affirmation or image.

❄ **Review the Validity:** Review the thoughts to examine their validity. Ask yourself: 'Is this right?', 'Does the situation justify such negative thoughts?', and 'Is the thought realistic?' Most of the time you will find that your thought process will alter from the negative to the positive.

❄ **The Right to Be Joyful:** Focus on your right to be happy rather than your justification to be angry or sad. Holding on to anger or sadness only weakens you. It's a choice you deliberately make.

❄ **Rephrase and Reject:** Reform each thought in terms of what you want in your life rather than what you don't want. For example, thoughts of affluence become 'I want to be well-off' as opposed to 'I don't want to be poor.'

❄ **Stop Worrying:** Examine the situation objectively. Determine what you can do to influence a positive outcome in the situation and act on it. Anything that you can't do means that you have no influence and worrying won't change that. When the situation comes to mind, remind yourself of the actions you took. Then change your thoughts to create a positive outcome.

❄ **Mental Hygiene:** Just as we take our daily bath and follow certain rules for physical hygiene, we need to re-enforce the rules of mental hygiene. Clearing the garbage and making place for the beautiful is what mental hygiene is all about. All it takes is a couple of moments a few times every day to repeat an empowering affirmation or review a positive image. This is a boost to your immune system, a mood lifter and a spiritual reconnection.

❄ **Using Spirituality:** Use your spiritual or religious beliefs to your advantage. Within these frameworks exist beliefs or practices to provide strength and encouragement. For example, 'What you focus on expands', or 'The Lord helps those who help themselves'. Belief is a very powerful motivator that will help to shape your thoughts. Therefore, foster positive and empowering beliefs.

❄ **Take Responsibility:** It is important for us to take the responsibility for our reactions to events and stop blaming others or situations. You may not have directly been responsible for an event, but you can choose how you react to it. This approach will awaken you to your ability to alter the effects of the situation rather than make you feel helpless and victimised.

❄ **Healthy Thoughts:** Your body lives out your thoughts. Whether you are experiencing a temporary or long-term illness, focus on all of the healthy, supporting systems of your body. Your body is composed of billions of cells, and out of these most are doing their jobs well. If you are well, then express gratitude to your body.

❄ **The De-Stress Routine:** Take time to de-stress daily. Even a couple of ten-minute breaks in the course of the day can have enormous benefits to your mind and body. Deep breathing, short meditations or regular stretching will relax the nervous system, slow down responses, calm the mind and put you back in touch with your body.

RECAP

- Spirituality is the science that teaches us to free and un-condition our minds.
- The mind is the most restless thing on the earth. It runs like an unbridled horse from one thought to the other.
- Our mind, body and spirit are an extremely sensitive, intricately balanced and interconnected system.
- What the mind focuses on becomes a part of our existence. Negative, angry, sad and self-defacing thoughts are toxic to your system. They are literally poisonous.
- Toxic thoughts can do as much damage to our system as a disease virus.
- It is essential to detoxify the mind in order to remain healthy and stress free.

PRAYER POWER

Prayers can heal. They are immensely powerful tools of healing. Earlier, it was only godmen and the gurus who advocated prayers in one's daily routine, but now the doctors are also suggesting that a regular prayer session could save your heart from falling prey to fatal diseases.

In a study conducted in 1997, it was found that Indians who prayed regularly were 70 per cent less likely to suffer from heart disease than those who didn't follow the daily prayer routine. Prayers and meditations have been an inherent discipline in the life of Indians, in the past. In fact, the connection between body and soul has existed in our culture for centuries. This connection was used by healers to cure people of most diseases, but with advancement of science and medicine, the importance of mind–body connection was ignored by most healers and doctors. We began following the western practitioners in our healing practices. As we progressed, we lost the vital wisdom that was followed by our sages and traditional healers. The natural herbs and medicines were replaced with antibiotics and western prescriptions. The resultant reactions to the antibiotics were discovered much later.

Prayers are a potent power that helps us cope with all kinds of adversities and negative forces in our lives. They are the salvation for depressed and hopeless beings.

The importance of the eastern medicine and cures was rediscovered by us only when the western world, after suffering from the ill effects of their own medicine, woke up and acclaimed them. All of a sudden there was clamour for all kinds of ancient eastern wisdom; from yoga to ayurveda and religion, everything was rediscovered by the Indians.

Praying has been a part of every Indian household for centuries. Thankfully, the practice of praying every evening is still followed by most families. With more evidence coming our way regarding the efficacy of prayers in healthy living, it is imperative that the younger generation be taught the benefits of following the footsteps of the older generations.

For several years, scientists and doctors have been researching on the link between prayers and a healthy life. Spiritual support groups have sprung up in the western countries to help the ailing people, especially the terminally ill. Tremendous recovery in some patients points to the power of prayers. The positive energy that is generated during the prayers has certainly a much more powerful effect than the scientists realise. We have just been exposed to the tip of the iceberg; the immense potentiality of praying has yet to be discovered. Today, there are more than a hundred medical colleges in the United States, which have a course, called Religious Traditions in Health Care. This subject is taught to the medical students and covers the correlation between spirituality and health. It also teaches about the major religions across the globe from a medical perspective.

Researchers are slowly unravelling the deep connection between spirituality and our body, through painstaking research. Some of the astounding facts that have been unveiled by them are:

Healthier Level of Blood Pressure: In a path-breaking finding, researchers found significant protective effects against high BP in men who are religious and pray regularly. One of the explanations could be that all activities that control stress are good for the heart and both prayers as well as chanting have a soothing effect on the mind. We suffer from high blood pressure because of the disturbed mind and when the same mind is calm, during prayers, it brings a healing effect on the heart and all other blood vessels.

General Sense of Well-Being and Happiness: Epidemiologist and author, Jeff Levin, conducted a study on old people and discovered that the old adults who are religious have fewer health problems and a better sense of well-being than those who were not religious. Well-being, again, depends on the state of our minds and souls. If the mind is calm and the soul satisfied, the physical benefits will definitely be available.

Recuperative Power: In a study conducted at the Dartmouth Medicine School, doctors found that patients who had gone through open-heart surgery and were religious had three times the chance of being alive after the first six months of surgery. Faith brings healing and when people have faith in their healer and the Supreme, they were more likely to survive the surgery and other medical problems than those who were sceptical.

Sturdy Hearts: In a study conducted in 1997, it was found that Hindus who pray regularly were 70 per cent less likely to have coronary heart disease. In Hindu belief, the heart is not just an organ for pumping blood, but also a compassionate and religious organ. We tend to involve emotions with the heart. A religious heart with positive emotions is, therefore, more likely to remain healthy.

Longer Life Expectancy: Studies show a 7-year difference between life expectancy of the believers and the non-believers.

Reduced Emotional and Psychological Ailments: Those who pray regularly are less likely to suffer from psychological and emotional problems like depression and anxiety. This could be due to several facts. One of them is the deep involvement with religion, which brings a sense of security to the person. This is especially true when people go through group religious practices like satsang and kirtan sessions where the group therapy works on a mental level.

De-stressing and Enhanced Immunity Benefits: Dr Herbert Benson of Harvard Medical School found that practices like meditation, prayer, tai chi and yoga reduce stress and enhance immunity. We all know that most ailments are related to the high levels of stress that people are going through, in modern times. Stress brings with it a lowered immunity level, besides the heart problems and other ailments. Prayer, yoga and meditation are very potent methods of de-stressing. Hence, they bring with them the allied health benefits.

But the prayer as we know it is just another means of asking for more from God. We get on our knees and beg for something, we do charity and ask for our wishes to be granted; we go to temples and ask for favours. That is not all, we promise to bribe God when the wish gets fulfilled. We tell God, 'Oh, God, let me get a good job and I will donate Rs.501 to your temple', or some such equally ridiculous thing. We trudge long distances when someone tells us about a temple, which houses a powerful deity who grants all kinds of boons.

This is not prayer. Prayers should be meant as genuine thanksgiving to God for having gifted us with precious life. It should be meant as praise to the almighty for giving us the little things that we take for granted. Only then can it bring peace and happiness to us. Or else, it remains a futile exercise.

RECAP

- Prayers are immensely powerful tools of healing.
- In a study conducted in 1997, it was found that Indians who prayed regularly were 70 per cent less likely to suffer from heart disease than those who didn't pray daily.
- Some of the benefits of prayers are: healthier level of blood pressure, general sense of well-being and happiness, de-stressing and enhanced immunity benefits and sturdy hearts.
- Better recuperative power, longer life expectancy, and reduced emotional and psychological ailments are also associated with regular praying habits.

RELAXATION AND THE ART OF FORGIVENESS

How often have we found ourselves saying, 'I will never forgive you for this'? Many times, I am sure right from our school days when we felt let down by a friend to the present day when we feel let down by the spouse. Whether in our careers or personal life, the unforgiving stance is a common occurrence. We brood over the so-called-wrongs committed by the people we trust and promise not to forget or forgive.

Nothing causes more stress and diminished output than the grudge we harbour against someone. It is our fault-finding and condemning others, as well as ourselves, that not only causes us stress but also has the potential of being injurious to our health. The grievances that we carry with us from old and new personal relationships can play a significant role in many of our illnesses.

Today, if there were a new medicine in the market, which promised to get rid of your different body aches, insomnia, and other problems, free of cost and without any side effects, we would all rush to buy it by the dozen. We would conveniently forget that most of these psychosomatic diseases are caused by anger, grievances, guilt and shame. We would forget that all these ailments are caused by our angry emotions and unforgiving thoughts.

Here is a ready-made panacea gifted by God. One, which costs nothing, has no side effects and works like a miracle, but we are not willing to use it. Forgiveness, the miracle cure, is available to all who want to exercise it. Besides mopping up all the ailments, it would gift us with a healthy and happy mind, totally guilt-free. As a bonus we would be granted physical fitness to go with it.

Holding on to grievances and unforgiving thoughts is like putting toxins into the mind. While none of us would consciously swallow poison, we continue to keep angry, toxic thoughts in our minds, which are lethal to our systems. Our emotions affect our immune system and every organ in the body. Holding on to bitterness and resentment is like slow poisoning.

Mounting evidence now suggests that not forgiving others may get you gallstones; if the problem pertains to the spouse, the stones form in the kidneys instead. The ensuing emotions and anger may involve back problems depending on whether the lack you feel is in emotional or material support.

If you have unrealistically high standards of judgment, which make it difficult for you to forgive, your nagging nature may give rise to complicated medical problems relating to liver and other digestive organs.

When we make the decision not to forgive, we are actually deciding to continue suffering. Why then do so many of us find it so difficult to forgive? When we forgive someone, it does not mean that we support the things he did. Forgiveness simply means that we have made the decision to heal our own minds by letting go of the hurtful past, a past that our anger and judgments cannot change.

My friend Sharad Rathore once narrated an incident to me. He had not spoken to his stepmother for years because he harboured a resentment against her for having replaced his mother's rightful place. Neither did he visit his father. He instigated the other siblings and did everything possible to make life difficult for them. For years, he avoided attending family functions and kept himself aloof from all ties. The simmering anger within him began to take a toll on his mental and physical health. Sharad knew that he had to bridge the differences with his family, but his ego prevented him from doing so.

It was on his daughter's betrothal that he realised that he wanted his father's blessings for her. Sharad personally went with the invitation to his father and begged for forgiveness. The old man was overwhelmed. Tears flowed from their eyes as they hugged each other lovingly and patched up the differences.

'From that day I was able to sleep peacefully,' says Sharad, about the reconciliation.

Forgiveness is the bridge to love, peace, happiness and well-being. It allows us to cleanse our souls of guilt, blame and shame. When we forgive, we transcend the barriers of ego and pompousness. We connect with that which is greater than our self and become better human beings. Nursing resentments turns us into shallow people.

Anita Kapoor is an example of how toxic thoughts affect the body. Five years ago, her husband was murdered by a business associate, who was later convicted of the murder and sentenced for life. Anita was not satisfied with the sentence. She believed that he had committed an unforgivable act and should have got a death sentence. She fought the case to the High Court. In the process, she spent more money than she had budgeted for; she also squandered precious energy and time than she could afford to do. She wanted revenge at all cost. The rage she harboured engulfed her mind.

Through the years, Anita developed an increasing number of medical problems. She lost her glorious hair, developed stones in the gall bladder and suffered from asthmatic and digestive problems. This was not all.

When the High Court turned down her appeal, she began to suffer from acute depression and neurotic state of mind, which required her to undergo psychotherapy.

It was during this phase that she met a spiritual teacher. She attended several workshops and realised that it was time she let go of her anger and vengeful thoughts, for her own good. On the suggestion of her spiritual guru, she made a symbolic gesture of forgiveness. By continued affirmations of her forgiveness, she was eventually able to recover from most of her ailments.

All the wise men and sages have known the power of forgiveness. It is said that there was a lady who always abused and pelted garbage on Prophet Mohammed whenever he passed her house. The Prophet never reacted to her abuses. One day, she failed to abuse him when he passed her house. Surprised, he climbed up the steps of a house to inquire about her health and well-being. The lady was stricken with guilt and remorse, and from that day she became an ardent follower of the Prophet.

Why Is It Difficult to Forgive?

Vengeful Thoughts: We carry thoughts of hatred because we blame others for the bad that befalls us. This illusion seems comforting. It does not require us to take any responsibility and allows us to judge others without letting ourselves be judged. It gives us a chance to become the object of sympathy and approval of others.

Fear of Being Mistaken: We fear that the other person may continue with his unwanted and irrational behaviour if we forgive. It is a baseless fear. There are more chances of a person understanding the foolishness of his action in the calm waters of forgiving silence than in the disturbed state of reactive behaviour. Your hatred, on the other hand, may make his behaviour look justified to him. So, if you really want him to change, practise forgiveness.

Programmed Behaviour: We expect others to behave the way we want. This may be unreasonable, but it can actually happen without any resistance, provided we surrender the desire and let people behave the way they have learnt to behave and let things happen the way they are bound to happen. We should be grateful to the universe for all that is happening to us. This is what is programmed in our best interests.

Grudges and Resentments: We continue to hold grudges against the people we presume to have wronged us. We refuse to accept that all that is happening to us is a result of the seeds sown by us, the way we process the behaviour of others and respond to any stimuli that we are exposed to. No one else is responsible for our unpleasant experiences. Our distress at others' behaviour reflects our own inner turmoil.

Labels: The fear of being labelled as weak, dumb and timid often stops us from forgiving. We think forgiveness is an excuse for escapism, inaction or cowardice and only those who cannot fight believe in forgiving. But there is an obvious difference between fearing and forgiving. Yes, there are people who disguise their fears as forgiveness. But your decision to forgive will not turn you into a coward. Moreover, why should we be ashamed of admitting that we cannot fight?

The Art of Forgiveness

Recognise that forgiveness is an act of strength, not weakness. Be open to the possibility of changing your beliefs about forgiveness.

- Choose to believe that holding on to grievances and unforgiving thoughts is choosing to suffer. Find no value in self-pity. Stop enjoying the feeling of being a victim.
- The events of the past cannot hurt you now, but your thoughts about the past can cause you immense distress and pain. Recognise that any emotional pain you feel this moment is caused only by your own thoughts. Remind yourself that

your anger and judgments can't change the past or punish someone else, but they can hurt you.

- It is no coincidence that the happiest people are those who choose not to judge and know the value of forgiveness. Recognise the value of giving up, not some, but all of your judgments.
- Ask yourself this question, 'Does holding on to my justified anger really bring me peace of mind?' Anger and peace, judgment and happiness do not occur at the same time. Recognise that holding on to anger will not bring you what your truly want. When you carry on with your grudges, you not only allow the other person to hurt you, but also let him control your life each moment you are affected by his thoughts.
- Once you truly recognise that your angry, unhappy thoughts about the past are poisoning your life, you will embrace forgiveness and know the meaning of love. Understand the fact that there is no point in punishing yourself for someone else's folly.
- Accept your past, forgive your past, and embrace the present and future with hope! There is no law forcing you to remain a victim of the past. Believe that forgiveness means trying to erase the wrongs of the past.
- When we stop trying to control others and focus instead on our own thoughts, we give ourselves the gift of freedom and peace. Choose to be happy rather than right. You strengthen your well-being. There are only losers in the game of war.
- Perhaps the greatest gift we have been given is the power to choose loving thoughts rather than angry ones. Your mind is not a dustbin that will remain unaffected by the trash you put into it. Treat it like a garden and it will blossom. Believe

that you have the power to choose the thoughts you put into your mind.

- Be willing to make peace of mind your only goal and believe that forgiveness is the key to happiness. Regardless of the chaos around us, we can know peace if that is our single goal. Choose not to let outside circumstances or people decide whether you will be happy. Anger, judgments and unforgiving thoughts make us suffer, and releasing them brings us joy. Believe that you have the power to choose the thoughts you put into your mind.
- Forgiving aligns us with the cosmic scheme through which we learn to accept that each event is there in our life because we need to learn from it.
- Forgiving is the essence of spirituality because it prepares us for our ultimate liberation from suffering. It requires the development of our ability to refrain from judging and to surrender ourselves to the natural unfolding of destiny.

RECAP

- Nothing causes more stress and diminished output than the resentment we harbour against someone.
- Not forgiving others may get you gallstones. The ensuing emotions and anger may aggravate or cause back problems.
- Holding on to bitterness and resentment is like slow poisoning.
- Anger and peace; judgment and happiness do not occur at the same time.

- It is no coincidence that the happiest people are those who choose not to judge and know the value of forgiveness.

CHAPTER FIVE

Recharging the Body, Mind and Soul

Relaxing the body, mind and spirit is one part of the game, but recharging it is an absolutely different ball game. If you love your car and don't want to give up on it when it is not functioning at its optimum level, what would you do? You would drive it into the nearest garage and ask for the best of the service persons to refurbish and repair your car. You would select carefully the colour you would like it to be repainted with, opt for the right kind of upholstery and fix the best music system you can find. After all this is over, just imagine the experience of driving your beloved car.

Our body is also something that requires tender loving care, rejuvenation and repair. Just as you make sincere efforts to do up your car, you need to listen to the body and make equally sincere effort to keep it in good shape. Make space for a de-stress day every week so that it keeps working at its optimum level.

A De-Stress Routine

A typical day for most people begins in a hurried manner

and this hurricane movement of the limbs, mind and spirit continues through the day, stressing out each and every cell of the body as well as mind. While there are many factors that contribute to stress, hurry and rush definitely remain a major cause of the unhealthy stress levels. The constant mental and physical stress eventually affects our health. The schedule given here is designed to break the stress pattern and bring about peace and tranquillity, even when the entire process is not completed.

To begin with the schedule it is best to opt for a day when you are not working and can take the day with a leisurely stride. Ideally, it would mean that you have the time and inclination to carry out the process. This is important because a working day would mean rushing against time, once again. Even if you were able to follow this routine on your non-working days, it would bring about a change in your mental and physical sense of well-being.

A Calming Wake Up

As opposed to your normal morning schedule, follow a slow, relaxed and calming wake-up routine. Take your time in bed after waking up. Luxuriate in the morning sounds that you do not have the time to hear on working days. Reach out and put on a CD of sacred chanting to create positive energy in your surroundings. Stretch your limbs slowly and feel the laziness ebb away as you smile to yourself. Slowly, wake up your muscles with the stretching exercises. Sit up on your bed and thank the Almighty for all that he has gifted you with.

Meditate

To ground yourself, sit in the lotus position on the floor and light an incense stick to create a peaceful aura around you. Aromatic candles, which soothe the mind, will also bring a sense of tranquillity. Even if you have never meditated, spend time with your inner thoughts. End the process with affirmations like 'I am calm and at peace with myself', 'This is a glorious day', 'Today is the happiest day of my life' and so on... This will set your mind on the right track. Follow it up with rejuvenating breath to detoxify your lungs. Practise pranayam for ten minutes in order to energise your systems and breathe life into them.

Live in the Moment

Let the day unwind as it does without any hurry or pre-planned schedule. If there are friends and relatives you have not communicated with for a long time, today is the day to do so. Ring them up, visit them or just spend the day with them. If you remain at home, put on soothing music, pull the curtains, light aromatic candles all around the house, place fresh flowers in vases and begin the next phase of actions.

An Aromatic Bath

It is time for a soothing aroma massage. Here is an anti-stress blend of essential oils that will pave the way for a calm day. 15 drops of clary sage, 10 drops lemon, and 5 drops lavender to be blended with an ounce of sweet almond oil – you can create this blend and keep in an air-tight jar. Take a few drops of it and enjoy a self-massage before your bath. Bathing with essential oils is a wonderfully synergistic combination. The relaxing properties of hot water compliment the effects of well-chosen essential oils. Aromatic baths can provide relief from stress and anxiety, assist with muscle pains. One of the most pleasant ways of using aromatic oils is to put 1–2 drops into a bath just before you get in; they form a thin film over the surface of the water, which coats and penetrates the skin while you lie in the heady aroma.

On the emotional level, several essences have quite remarkable effects in helping to keep the mood in balance. The best anti-depressant oil is undoubtedly bergamot, and this can be used to ward off low vitality at times of stress and depression. A note of caution though – bergamot increases sensitivity to the sun, so do not overuse before exposure to bright sunlight. Other mood elevators are neroli (or orange blossom), jasmine, melissa and rose.

De-Stressing Sustenance

In a major breakthrough scientists have discovered the link between stress and overeating leading to weight gain. They also found that stressed-out people often turn to food for solace and eat with almost an endless appetite. A surprise finding also led them to study the release of hormones during stress-ridden phases. The results showed that these hormones had a major role to play in the weight-gain process.

To stress-proof your diet avoid foods that release sugar into the bloodstream too quickly and cause wide fluctuations. These include highly-processed sugary foods and white starches, such as white rice, bread and pasta.

The danger zone for stress overeating is mid-afternoon to evening – eating a substantial, balanced breakfast and lunch and a healthy mid-afternoon snack can combat stress-induced cravings.

For some people cooking can be a cathartic experience, but for some it could bring about stress. If you are the kind who finds cooking a calming experience, go ahead and pamper yourself with exotic food, but if you don't like spending time in the kitchen, order for home delivery of your most favourite dishes. Food can relieve anxiety and have a calming influence on your mind. Certain foods can act as tranquillisers and help you retain your equanimity.

Consuming the right food can bring a calming effect on your mind and body. Among the recommended food are lettuce, which contains beta-carotene, potassium, vitamin C and some calcium. Herbalists often use it as a calming food. Yoghurt and other forms of milk contain tryptophan, which the brain converts into the soothing chemical serotonin. The complex carbohydrates found in brown rice may increase the level of serotonin, known for its calming properties. High-carbohydrate root vegetables can help boost serotonin, the stress-busting and tranquillising hormone.

Ginger is known to be calming to a stressed or upset digestive system.

Natural Panacea

Nature is one of the most de-stressing things that God has provided us. A walk in the park amidst greenery can do much more than any other anti-stress exercise. The harmony that is seen in nature can easily be transported to your own self if you let your natural instincts take over. Sit on a bench in the park and observe the various hues of green around you, watch the butterflies darting from flower to flower, enjoy the sunshine-brightened glory of nature all around you. You may never have noticed the delicate petals of the flowers opening up to greet you, or the merry laughter of the children around you. Just spending time observing these things can bring joy to a heart and serve as the most rejuvenating of all therapies.

Chant – how long has it been since you chanted the sacred mantras? To savour the healing effect of the simple Aum, sit cross-legged on a mat, close your eyes and take a deep breath. Chant Aum from the deep recess of your belly, bringing it up as energy till it reaches your lungs. You will feel the reverberation of the notes as you chant, cleansing and energising you.

Follow up the chanting process with a visualisation exercise. Sit comfortably on the floor or in a straight-backed chair with your palms facing upwards. Inhale deeply and close your eyes. Exhale and inhale deeply for a couple of minutes, sense the pure oxygen filtering into your system. Now visualise the colour green surrounding your heart and concentrate on its beats. You will begin to feel all residual tensions leaving your body even as the calmness floats into your heart.

No matter what you do for the rest of the day, just follow these procedures carefully during the time you can spare for them. Remember to meditate for a few minutes before you go to bed. That will ensure a good and sound sleep while preparing you to face the ordeal for the next few days. Reserve at least one weekend in a month to follow the above practice, and you are likely to remain at your efficient best without getting stressed.

Powerful Relaxation Techniques

Some of us are more stressed than others. It is either their jobs or lives that may be causing them to bear the burden of additional stress, but there are ways to combat the tension through some simple exercises. These simple breathing techniques can be performed for immediate stress release.

1. Sitkari (Folded-Tongue Pranayam)

- Sit in a comfortable posture, with an erect spine. Exhale from both nostrils.
- Fold the tongue backwards and press the tip of the tongue by the hard palate, leaving narrow openings on either side of the tongue. Inhale through these side openings making a hissing sound.
- Allow the breath to be stopped with ease.
- Exhale slowly and continuously through both the nostrils.
- Then allow the breath to stop with ease and release.
- Repeat several times.

2. Sitali (Beak-Tongue Pranayam)

- Sit in a comfortable posture, with an erect spine. Exhale from both nostrils
- Fold up the sides of the partially-protruded tongue so as to form a long, narrow tube resembling the beak of a bird. Press the lips round the tongue to narrow further the passage.

- Inhale, making a hissing noise and perceive the cooling effect of the air as it passes through the tongue.
- Allow the breath to be stopped effortlessly.
- Exhale through both nostrils.
- Then allow the breath to be held comfortably before the next inhalation.
- Repeat the cycle several times.

3. Sadanta (Suction-through-Teeth Pranayam)

- Sit in a comfortable posture, with an erect spine. Exhale from both nostrils.
- Press the upper teeth on the lower ones.
- Suck in the air through the gaps between the teeth in a slow and continuous manner.
- Allow the breath to stop automatically.
- Exhale through both nostrils.
- Hold the breath comfortably for a while before the next inhalation.
- Repeat the cycle several times.

All the three pranayam exercises are called cooling pranayams because they cause cooling to the bodily systems. They help in calming down the mind by eliminating mental anxiety and tension, increase the resistance to diseases, especially of the respiratory nature.

Some Quick Relaxers

A Shoulder Shrug: With arms at your sides, lift your shoulders up towards your ears as far as they will go, then pull them down as far as they will go. Repeat five times. This will drain out the stress from your shoulder and neck region.

An Effective Sigh: Sigh as loudly and deeply as you can. Then inhale deeply, as fully as possible. This is a very effective remedy for immediate focusing of the mind and instant de-stressing.

Smile Therapy: Remind yourself of a happy event and let the smile travel from your face down to your heart. If possible laugh aloud. Laughter is a physical and mental relaxer.

Neck Rollers: Sit straight with the shoulders relaxed. Gently roll your neck down towards your right shoulder as far as it can go, return to the top and roll down to the left. Repeat five times. The roll will take the stress off the neck muscles.

Magical Massage: Using first and second fingers of both hands, gently make small circular motions (clockwise with your right fingers, anti-clockwise with your left). Start the movements above the inner eyebrows and gradually move the fingers across your forehead to the temples then, gently, down your eyes, across the cheekbones to your nose. With regular massage, the stress lines around your eyes will fade away.

Recap

- For a completely de-stressing day, play music that has an expansive spirit.
- Scent the air with essence of ylang-ylang, either by lighting aromatic candles or spraying it around.
- A few drops of lavender oil on your pillow can work magically to soothe your brain.
- Four to six drops of neroli, marjoram or chamomile in the bath can work wonders in sedating your body and brain. An aromatherapy

massage with these oils can also refresh and rejuvenate the body and mind.

- Chant and meditate, visualise and stretch. Scatter flowers all around the house.
- Eat food that is de-stressing and light.
- Spend time outdoors, communing with nature and sharing the joys of the being in harmony with God's creation.
- Live in the moment. Abstain from hurrying or rushing – take time to be with your inner self.

Rejuvenation and Energising Exercises

Given below are some exercises based on acupressure to soothe the mind and body. They are equally effective in energising and rejuvenating the body.

- There is a spot on the inside of your ankle bone, just four fingers above the bone, which is actually the spot for bringing a soporific effect on the body and mind. Press the spot with your thumb for about fifteen seconds. Do this on the spot on both the left ankle and the right one, for immediate relaxation.
- For an instant sleep-inducing effect, sit on a flat surface and bend one leg. Place your elbow on your kneecap for support and exert a slight pressure on the bridge of your nose with the thumb. Keep the pressure for about fifteen to twenty seconds before releasing.
- Locate the spot on your wrist where there is a small depression just under the palm. Now draw a line from the left little finger down to this area on the wrist. Press with the thumb for about twenty seconds and release. Now, repeat the same procedure on the other wrist. This exercise

is likely to bring immediate effect in getting you relaxed.

- One of the most effective pressure treatments geared towards clearing the mind is to use it on the point between your eyebrows in the middle of your forehead. Using one of your index fingers apply firm pressure at this spot, while making small rotations both clockwise and anticlockwise over the point. Hold for about three minutes.
- The acupoint located in the fleshy part of the hand between the thumb and forefinger (close to where the bones meet), helps stimulate mental awareness of the world around us. Hold your left hand, palm down, in front of you, supporting it with the fingers of your right hand. Spread your thumb and forefinger. With your right thumb apply firm downward pressure on the acupoint. Hold for about two minutes. Repeat the same process on the other hand.

  Warning: do not stimulate this acupoint during pregnancy.
- The acupoint located just below the ball of your foot, a third of the way along the sole, is the spot that can be used to boost vitality and relieve fatigue. Sit with your right foot on your left knee. Apply pressure to the acupoint with your right thumb for two minutes. Repeat on your left foot.
- Most of us find it difficult to meditate because we can't concentrate. With increasing stress levels concentration becomes more and more difficult. To improve mental alertness, use the acupoint located in the groove above the upper lip. Apply gentle pressure with the tip of the index finger on the point for about three minutes. Keep your finger perpendicular to the groove.

Note: acupressure works well if you manage to keep the body relaxed and breathe regularly throughout the session. It is natural to experience a slight tingling sensation in the area you are massaging. It is advisable to discontinue the pressure if it becomes painful.

Allied Relaxation Techniques

There are many approaches to relaxation. All these methods are easy to use and equally powerful in producing results. But we are all very different from each other, so we may find some techniques working better for us. If technique A works for your friend, it is not necessary that it will work equally effectively on you. It has been found that techniques using imagery are very helpful to some people, but not useful to others. Sometimes you may find that a particular technique works for a while and then becomes ineffective because you have got used to it. If that happens, it is time to try something else. You may have to try several techniques to see what works for you. Permutation and combinations are also possible. If you find that working with an amalgam of two techniques works better for you, by all means combine the techniques.

The Body Scan

Founded by Jon Kabat-Zinn, the director of the Stress Reduction Clinic at the University of Massachusetts Medical Centre, the body scan is a technique that helps you relax your entire body. Although it is recommended that you do it lying down, you could perform the exercise in any position that you find comfortable.

Take a deep breath and feel the movements in your body as you inhale and exhale. Begin by spending a few minutes focusing on your breath, visualising it going deeply into your body and then out again.

After several minutes, direct your attention to the toes of one foot, becoming aware of any sensations you feel there. Be aware of the twitching or itching or restlessness in that part of your body. Do not try to relax your toes, just concentrate your attention on them. Strangely, just by focusing your attention on them, you will find that you are able to bring about relaxation. If you find your mind has wandered, bring your attention back to your breathing and to the toes, once again. After about half a minute, move your attention to the bottom of the foot. Again, don't try to relax it, just become aware of any sensations that might be present. Then move gradually on to the top of the foot, the ankle and the calf. The attention should move very slowly from one part to the other, without any hurry or disruption. If your mind wanders, bring it back to your breath, let it stabilise and then move on to the part of your body you are focusing on.

Gradually work your way through the whole body, moving up one leg to the hip, and then towards the other leg starting with the toes. Then move on to the stomach, chest and back, followed by the hands, arms and shoulders. Lastly, focus on the neck, jaw, mouth, eyes and scalp. The important point is to: (a) focus your attention on one body part at a time without consciously trying to relax it; and (b) return your attention to the breath and then the body, when your mind wanders.

The Relaxation Response

Dr Herbert Benson of Harvard developed the technique of relaxation response, which produces a state of deep rest in the mind and body. The technique, quite similar to meditation, involves keeping your attention on a point of focus, usually a word that you repeat silently to yourself. It can be an affirmation or a mantra. As you focus on your mental device, you will experience distracting thoughts, images or feelings. When you find that you have become distracted, simply return to your point of focus. Do this whenever you discover that your attention has drifted away from your point of focus.

How would you know if you have been able to accomplish the relaxation response technique?

If you were able to generate a pleasant state of mind and calm the thought process, you have been able to accomplish the right result. For example, after performing the technique, does your body and mind experience the same pleasure as it might have while lying on the beach? Does it experience the sense of detached relaxation you generally feel just before falling asleep? If the answer to both these questions is 'yes', you have successfully performed the relaxation response technique.

The first thing to do is to get comfortable. Go to a quiet place where you won't be disturbed for some time, assume a comfortable posture and close your eyes. (Sitting is generally preferable, but not essential.)

Now, relax your body. Beginning at your feet and moving gradually up to your head, relax the muscles in your body. You might include in your scan of the body your feet, ankles, calves, thighs, stomach, chest, back, hands, arms, shoulders, neck, jaw, mouth, eyes, scalp.

Become aware of your breathing. Spend a short time following your breath. Feel it come in through your nose and go out through your mouth. Once you have got in the rhythm with your breath, concentrate on your point of focus. Your focus can be a word like 'relax' or Aum, a prayer, a symbol or even a feeling. On each exhalation, repeat the word or focus on your chosen symbol or feeling.

Let this continue for ten to fifteen minutes. If you find yourself distracted from your point of focus, return your attention to your breathing and your focus word or phrase. After you finish, sit quietly for a few minutes. Let the awareness of your surroundings filter back to your mind before you begin your activities.

Guided Imagery

Guided imagery uses our ability to create scenes in our mind as a way to distract us from worry and help us relax. Imagery has been found to be a powerful tool of relaxation. This technique can be performed in three steps.

1. Focusing: Find a comfortable and quiet place. Sit on the floor and close your eyes. Watch your breath as you inhale and exhale. Continue to focus on your breathing for a few minutes and feel your tension release.

2. Visualising: Visualise a scene in which you can become engrossed. It could be lolling on the beach with the blue sea waves kissing your toes, walking through a lovely forest or even something from the past like remembering a place that gives your warm, pleasant feelings. What you visualise as the setting is not as important as how the scene you choose makes you feel. Involve as many of your senses as you can. The more senses you use, the more relaxing the scene will be. If you are at the beach, see and hear the waves crashing one after another on the sand, feel the warmth of the sun on your face and the wind against your skin, smell the ocean. If you are in a forest, smell the pine needles, hear the birds call and the water babble in the stream, see the soft light coming down through the branches of the trees. The idea is to picture a scene in such detail that you feel comfortable, safe and relaxed, so that your frustrations and worries fall away only to be replaced by a feeling of tranquillity and calm.

3. Returning: After 10 to 15 minutes, gradually bring your attention back to your body and the present surroundings. Remain in it for some time and when you feel comfortable, open your eyes.

It usually takes a while (at least several weeks of regular practice) to develop skill in using a technique, so allow some time before expecting results. To be fair, you should practise four or five times a week, setting aside for each session 10 to 20 minutes when you won't be disturbed. Learning concentration is a common problem when doing a relaxation practice. The mind tends to wander, so having patience is necessary.

There are many good relaxation and meditation tapes available today. Some have step-by-step instructions to lead you through a relaxation procedure, while others have music or relaxing sounds from nature. You may want to use such tapes or record your own from the techniques described above. Finally, if relaxation makes you anxious or seems unpleasant, try other stress reduction techniques.

Time spent in natural surroundings is also a natural way to soothe and heal the mind. You can bring nature into your home with fresh-cut flowers, live plants, natural sunlight and the sounds of birds and water. You can walk amongst the trees, mountains and by clean rivers, absorbing nature at its purest.

If you cannot create this feeling at home or outside, just imagine the following: 'Walking barefoot through grass, feeling the coolness and moisture of the morning mountain dew, stopping by a clear, fresh stream falling over smooth rocks. Dip your toes in the water and listen to the voice of the mountains. Allow the light and warmth of the sun to permeate you. Breathe in the pure, clean and cool air. Now imagine night is falling. The moon is full and round. Gaze up at the myriad stars drifting off into the solar system. Float back to earth once again to walk barefoot through the grass and feel the morning dew between your toes.'

A Stress-Releasing Technique

This is a simple exercise that can be performed within a few minutes, anywhere. The benefits include the ebbing of pain, stress and anxiety, and at the same time, this cleanses the whole of the physical body. It is especially useful for people who suffer from debilitating aches and pains.

- Find yourself a quiet corner, so that you will be able to relax without any disturbance.
- To relax your body, gently shake your feet and legs, hands and arms in turn, and finish by slowly turning your head from side to side.
- Breathe deeply three times. Sigh deeply if you are not able to exhale fully.
- Turn your awareness within. Focus your awareness on the skin that covers your body. Visualise it as à silken covering or a velvet coverlet. You can use a soothing colour to give realism to the visual effect.

- Visualise the smooth silk layer being topped with soft sponge that is absorbing all the pain, stress and anxiety.
- Now begin unwrapping the sponge that has soaked in all the pain, stress and anxiety from your body. Begin at the crown of your head moving downwards till you have pulled it down to your feet. This is the casing that contains all the aches and pains.
- Visualise burning or burying the sponge with the absorbed toxins. You are now rid of all the ills that hounded you.
- All that remains on your skin is the soft and beautiful silk, free of all kinds of pains.
- Use this exercise as frequently as you want. It really works!

A Visualisation Exercise

I am going to take you on a walk through the garden of peace, love, contentment and serenity. By taking this imaginary walk, you will be able to soothe your nerves and calm your mind within a few minutes. As we walk, we will leave behind the worries, noises and problems of the world and delve deeper into the realm of spirituality and happiness.

You can record this in a tape and play it whenever you want to relax. Visualise the scenes as the words dictate. Take your own time to unwind. Don't read it out fast and get done with it. The entire exercise must take at least fifteen minutes. Give sufficient pause in between. The intervening silence will allow you the time and space to use your visualisation.

Lie down in a quiet place, preferably a darkened room. Close your eyes and take a deep breath. Imagine for a moment that you are strolling into a heavenly garden. This very large garden is filled with fruit trees, and endless shrubs covered with colourful flowers. As you stroll down a winding path, you come upon a marble bench on which you can rest. The flowers that are all around and above you seem to slowly dance in the cool breeze.

As you look out over all the flowers, it's like looking over rolling waves of colour as the soft wind gently moves them back and forth. You inhale the floral fragrance deeply, and that fills you with peace and contentment. The birds above you seem to drift and float effortlessly in the breeze. The songs of their call seem to help you float deeply into a state of total relaxation. There are squirrels scurrying about gathering some of the nuts on the ground. Above you a few puffy white clouds slowly dance across the deep blue sky, and you can feel yourself drift into an inner peacefulness as the sunlight touches your face. The golden sunlight stands for everything that's good in life such as love, peace, harmony, and you can feel the warmth of the sunlight beginning to relax your entire body.

Allow this feeling of relaxation fill your entire body. Just think about relaxing every muscle in your body from the top of your head to the tips of your toes. Let go and relax. Shift the focus of your mind to experience the comfort your body is beginning to feel. Inhale and exhale deeply with a sigh. Focus on your breathing; become aware of the rhythm of your breathing and relax your breathing for a moment.

Be aware of any normal sounds around you. These sounds are unimportant... discard them... whatever you hear from now on will only help to relax you. And, as you slowly inhale, breathe in pure relaxing energy. As you exhale, release any tension, any stress from any part of your body, mind and thought; just let that stress go. Just feel any stressful thoughts rushing through your mind, feel them begin to wind down, wind down and relax...

Allow all the muscles in your face, especially your jaw, relax. Part your teeth slightly to relax this area. This is a place where tension and stress gather; so be sure and relax your jaw and feel that relaxation go into your temples, and relax the muscles in your temples, and as you think about relaxing these muscles, they will relax. Feel them relax, and as you relax, you'll be able to just drift and float into a deeper and deeper level of total relaxation... You will continue to relax... and now let all of the muscles in your forehead relax.

Feel those muscles smoothen, and rest your eyes. Just imagine your eyelids feeling comfortable and getting heavy, heavier and relaxed, and now let all of the muscles in the back of your neck and shoulders relax, feel a heavy, heavy weight being lifted off your shoulders and you feel relieved, lighter and more relaxed. And all of the muscles in the back of your neck and shoulders relax, and feel that soothing relaxation go down your back, down... to the lower part of your back, and those muscles.

Let go, and with every breath you inhale just feel your body drifting, floating, down, deeper, down deeper into total relaxation. Let your muscles go, relaxing more and more. Let all of the muscles in your shoulders, running down your arms to your fingertips relax. And let your arms feel so heavy, so comfortable, so relaxed. And now you inhale once again and relax your chest muscles. And now as you exhale, feel your stomach muscles relax. As you exhale, relax all of the muscles in your stomach, let them go, and all of the muscles in your legs, feel them relax and all the muscles in your legs, so completely relaxed right to the tips of your toes. Notice how very comfortable your body feels, just drifting and floating, deeper and deeper, into total relaxation.

And as you are relaxing deeper and deeper, imagine you are standing at the summit of a beautiful hill. Down below lies a serene marble palace. You are just ten steps away from the beautiful palace – your own safe haven. In a moment, you can begin to imagine taking a gentle step down, down the hill towards the palace. Count each step as you glide down on light steps. Imagine your body getting deeper into relaxation... deeper with each step... feel your body relax, more and more, feel it just drift down, down with each step, and relax even deeper.

Ten, relax even deeper... Nine, more relaxed with each step... Eight... Seven... Six... Five... Four... Three... Two... and One... deeper, relaxed. You are almost there now... you are relaxed. Breathe deeply and relax... Imagine yourself there, and feel the sense of peace flow through you as you sit down on a marble bench near a large window looking out at a beautiful garden... You experience a sense of well-being... Enjoy these positive feelings... And keep them with you... And these positive feelings will stay with you and grow stronger and stronger each day as you continue to relax... Take a deep breath, and drift over like the clouds. You are drifting into the realm of your subconscious. And it is here that you can hear the voice of your own heart. It is here that you can just sit and enjoy the simple expression of your own being.

And as you slowly begin coming back, travelling back to your full waking consciousness, you can bring back with you this relaxed feeling and all that was positive, and bright and interesting, and important. Returning through the levels of your mind to full consciousness. You will notice you're feeling much better than before. You will be wide-awake, clear headed, refreshed and happy. Slowly count from one to ten... At the count of ten, open your eyes, be wide-awake, clear headed, feeling fine. Begin your count now.

One: coming back very slowly.

Two: coming out very slowly now.

Three: coming up.

Four: feel the life energies returning throughout your being.

Five: feel total normalisation and perfect equilibrium.

Six: reenergised.

Seven: coming up to your full potential.

Eight: fully reoriented into the present.

Nine: revitalised.

Ten: Open your eyes... you're feeling great.

CHAPTER SIX

Assessment Exercises

Here are a few tests to help you find your bearing in the world of stress. You could take them lightly or seriously. If you take them seriously, they would act as indicators of the areas where improvement is needed. Whatever be your approach, these tests are geared to help you cope with life situations that sometimes seem overwhelmingly oppressing.

Are You Stressed?

- Are you a perfectionist?
- Do you feel a constant pressure to achieve?
- Do you criticise yourself when you're not perfect?
- Do you feel you haven't done enough no matter how hard you try?
- Do you give up pleasure in order to be the best in everything you do?

- Does your self-esteem depend on everyone else's opinion of you? Do you sometimes avoid assignments because you're afraid of disappointing your boss?
- Are you better at caring for others than caring for yourself?
- Do you keep most negative feelings inside to avoid displeasing others?

If the answer to all these questions is a 'yes', then the bad news is that you are a victim of stress. Maybe you already know that. So what do you do? It is not going to be an easy task but you'll have to make the effort to change your attitude.

Recognise These Stress Symptoms

1. The forehead is creased with frown lines.
2. The upper end of the neck is stiff and sore, and you can feel the knotted muscles on either side of the neck.
3. The jaw is stiff and the teeth clenched.
4. The scalp is tight.
5. The breathing is shallow and given to hyperventilation.
6. Toes are generally curled up inside the shoes.
7. Heartburn is a common problem.
8. Gestures like drumming the fingers on the desk, scratching the nose and patting the hair is a regular action.

If you connect these statements with yourself, dear friend, you are stressed.

Assess Your Stress Level

How do I know how stressed I am? Have I reached the danger zone, or am I a borderline case? These are some of the questions that bother most minds. We want to push our luck and heed only when we reach the danger mark.

Although everyone suffers from stress, there are some of us who are in the danger zone and need to examine his or her life from a fresh perspective. How do you know that you've reached an unhealthy level of stress?

Basically stress causes three kinds of symptoms – emotional, behavioural and physical. Here is checklist to help you decide if you have reached the danger mark of stress.

1. Are you constantly worrying or anxious?
2. Do you feel a sense of confusion and suffer from an inability to concentrate or make decisions?
3. Do you feel ill often?
4. Do you feel out of control or overwhelmed by events?
5. Does your mood swing too violently?
6. Do you suffer from depression, frustration or feel a sense of hostility quite often?
7. Or is it a sense of helplessness, impatience and irritability that is your problem?
8. Is there a sense of restlessness that shows up in your behaviour?
9. Have you noticed yourself becoming more lethargic in the recent times?
10. Do you experience difficulty sleeping?
11. Have you begun drinking more alcohol and smoking more than usual?
12. Is there a change in your eating habits?
13. Have been experiencing a reduction in your sex drive?
14. Do you talk too fast or too loud?
15. Have you begin fiddling and twitching, biting your nail, grinding your teeth, drumming fingers, pacing, etc.?
16. Have people been complaining about your bad mood, irritability or aggression?
17. Have you taken to being defensive or over-critical?
18. Do you overreact or react emotionally?

19. Have you noticed yourself being unreasonably negative, making less-realistic judgements, becoming more forgetful, making more mistakes, being more accident prone?
20. Have you begun taking less interest in your personal appearance?

For each 'yes', give yourself 2 marks and 0 mark for 'no'. If you score more than 20, it is time to sit up and take notice. More than 24 is bad; 32 and above indicates a dangerously high level of stress.

The first six questions are related to emotional symptoms of stress while the rest of them fall under behavioural or physical symptoms. These symptoms of stress should not be taken in isolation; other factors could cause them, too.

How Forgiving Are You?

Here is a test to determine your forgiveness quotient.

1. When a colleague stabs you in the back, you
   a. Ignore and go ahead with your job
   b. Challenge him
   b. Plan to get back at him at a later date
2. If the same colleague needs your help another day, do you
   a. Willingly help him out
   b. Make excuses
   c. Refuse bluntly
3. Your special friend does not turn up for the date
   a. You sulk for days, refusing to patch up
   b. Throw a tantrum and break up
   c. Talk over the reason for the let down
4. How would you react to someone who tormented you during your early life, if you meet him years later?
   a. Remember the slight and reject the person
   b. Begin afresh
   c. Get sarcastic and remind him about the unpleasant incident

5. Rejection could cause you to
   a. Introspect and improve
   b. Find excuses
   c. Carry grudges forever
6. Your colleague gets the promotion that is denied to you. Would you
   a. Run him down at every opportunity insinuating he has got it through unfair means
   b. Hint at favouritism
   c. Accept the situation with good grace and congratulate the colleague
7. You go through a divorce/break-up and end up
   a. Hating the spouse
   b. Understand that it is a two way street but avoid contact
   c. Maintain cordial relationship with the ex-spouse
8. Your rival makes it to a place you were dreaming about
   a. You find it in your heart to feel happy for him
   b. Ignore and simmer
   c. Backbite about unfairness of life
9. After a serious squabble with the spouse
   a. Do you find it difficult to say 'sorry' and take the first step towards reconciliation
   b. Smile and say 'sorry'
   c. Carry a cold war for weeks
10. A person you don't like goes through a bad phase
    a. You gloat over his misfortunes
    b. Feel genuinely sorry and want to help him out
    c. Remain aloof
11. You lose out a big project to your friend
    a. Congratulate him
    b. Break the friendship
    c. Turn cold to him
12. Your reaction to partiality of your parents towards your sibling
    a. Jealousy
    b. Detached
    c. Amused tolerance

Check Your Score

1. a -3
   b -2
   c -1
2. a -3
   b -2
   c -1
3. a -2
   b -1
   c -3
4. a -1
   b -3
   c -2
5. a -3
   b -2
   c -1
6. a - 1
   b -2
   c -3
7. a -1
   b -2
   c -3
8. a -3
   b -2
   c -1
9. a -2
   b -3
   c -1
10. a -1
    b -3
    c -2
11. a -3
    b -1
    c -2
12. a -1
    b -2
    c -3

Verdict

0–4: If you have scored between 0 and 5, you are absolutely relentless in your attitude. You never forgive. Let me not spell it out, but you are vengeful and unforgiving, and that is really a terrible way to be. You exist for revenge. I would relocate to Mars if I had upset you. The word 'forgive' or the phrase 'forgive and forget' do not exist in your dictionary. What you need to understand is that being vindictive will ruin your sense of peace. One forgives for one's benefit and not for the others'. You can never find happiness till you learn to forgive. It will definitely do you good to let the past remain in the past. Get on with life; it is too short for vengeance and vendetta. Do yourself a favour, begin forgiving.

5–9: That's a very realistic score. It shows you are human. We all find it difficult at times to forgive the ones who harm us. Eventually, we succumb to the temptation of living life peacefully and forgive the enemies. We get hurt, we react, and we make our displeasures evident. Yet we understand the logic of letting bygones be bygones without allowing unpleasant incidents to prey on our mind. It is intelligent not to allow the sores to fester. Forgiveness requires courage, and you have it in you. You are on the right path. Carry on!

10–12: Are you sure, you didn't cheat? It seems too good a score to be honest. Anyway, you are a very fine specimen of the human breed – forgiving, generous and gentle. There is a strong streak of spirituality in your personality. Though it is quite unbelievable for a person to be so good, there must be some people on this planet who have the guts to forgive without feeling regret. You are the one who will sleep peacefully at night, secure in the knowledge that your heart doesn't have to suffer guilt pangs at wrong doing. Hats off to you!

What about Leisure?

Leisure and relaxation are two sides of the same coin. It is important to make time for leisure if you want to be completely relaxed. The problem with most of us is that we have forgotten the meaning of leisure. Perhaps we have no time to call our own, lost in the jungle of tremendous activity as we are. Here is a test geared to tell you whether you are spending enough time for leisure.

1. Do you have at least half an hour of quiet time to yourself each day?

   Yes   No

   A   B

2. Are you always running short of time and snapping at everyone?

   No   Yes

   A   B

3. Do you feel you haven't achieved all you wanted to, at the end of the day?
   No Yes
   A B
4. Do most days give you a feeling of being stressed?
   No Yes
   A B
5. Do you suffer from stress-elevated blood pressure?
   No Yes
   A B
6. Do you have great difficulty in enjoying a vacation?
   No Yes
   A B
7. Do you feel a week after an enjoyable vacation that it never happened?
   No Yes
   A B
8. Do you have time for conversation with the people whose company you enjoy?
   Yes No
   A B
9. When you have time for leisure do you not know what to do with yourself?
   No Yes
   A B
10. Do you have a group of friends and family who support your leisure-time needs?
    Yes No
    A B
11. Is your leisure time scheduled too tightly for your true enjoyment?
    No Yes
    A B

Your score

Number of As

8–9: That's perfect! You have taken care to keep some time aside for leisure.

7–9: Not so bad. Try getting some more time to yourself.

4–6: Your leisure time could do with a little increase.

2–3: Quite bad. You must make an earnest effort to include more leisure time in your daily routine.

Less than 2: You just don't know the meaning of leisure.

While you are at it, make your own list of pleasures large or small. All you have to do now is to enjoy them – but don't forget the rules: include nothing except your own, true, real, deep pleasure. Don't let other people or outside influences dissuade you. Don't feel guilty for your pleasure time.

Are You a Type A Personality?

1. You have an appointment with your dentist, but he is busy with another patient and keeps you waiting for an hour.
   (a) You fret and fume and pick up a row with the receptionist.
   (b) You stomp off, deciding to return another day.
   (c) You wait for your turn with acceptance.
2. You are waiting at the airport and there is an announcement that the flight has been delayed indef initely due to technical reasons. You have a meeting to attend at your destination.
   (a) You demand an explanation at the airlines counter and threaten to make an issue.
   (b) After deferring the meeting, you buy the book you had wanted to read and settle down to finish it while waiting for the flight.
   (c) You make efforts to find if there are alternative flights to reach your destination in time to catch the meeting.

3. Your watch has gone for repair and you have to do without it for a day.
   (a) You feel lost without it and borrow one from your friend.
   (b) You are happy not to be tied by time for a day.
   (c) You try to find another shop that would repair it within a couple of hours.
4. You are standing outside the multiplex with tickets in your hand. The movie has already begun, but your girlfriend hasn't turned up. She is not reachable on her mobile either.
   (a) You decide to wait for another five minutes and then go in irrespective of whether she turns up or not.
   (b) You decide to wait till she arrives.
   (c) You return home and plan to have it out with her the next time you meet.
5. At a supermarket, you carefully tally the bill with the items you have purchased.
   (a) Always
   (b) Sometimes
   (c) Never
6. If you are short-changed by the cab driver who insists that he does not have change
   (a) You ignore the amount.
   (b) You insist on the change.
   (b) You have a verbal duel with the driver.
7. If you are given a choice between a job with job satisfaction and a job with bigger salary
   (a) You would settle for job satisfaction.
   (b) You would take up the one with higher salary.
   (b) You would take the one with higher salary but curse it for not giving you the satisfaction.
8. Are you a perfectionist?
   (a) Only sometimes
   (b) Always
   (c) No

9. You have been planning for a vacation for a long time. After you have made all the bookings and travel arrangements, there is a rush job that needs to be completed and the boss requests you to defer your plans
   (a) You agree easily.
   (b) You resent the change in plans.
   (c) You are absolutely livid. Although you change your plans, you give vent to your feelings by kicking the furniture around.
10. Some guests arrive unexpectedly just when you are about to set out for a movie.
   (a) You are absolutely mad and find it difficult to hide your anger.
   (b) You reconcile yourself to the change in plan grudgingly and entertain the guests.
   (c) You take the change in your stride and are happy to spend time with the guests.

The Score

1. (a) - 3, (b) -2, (c) - 1
2. (a) - 3, (b) -1, (c) - 2
3. (a) - 2, (b) -1, (c) - 3
4. (a) - 3, (b) -1, (c) - 2
5. (a) - 3, (b) -2, (c) - 1
6. (a) - 1, (b) -2, (c) - 3
7. (a) - 1, (b) -3, (c) - 2
8. (a) - 2, (b) -3, (c) - 1
9. (a) - 1, (b) -2, (c) - 3
10. (a) - 3, (b) -2, (c) - 1

The Verdict

25–30: You definitely belong to the Type A Club, and believe me it is no great distinction. You possess all the characteristics that will lead you to hypertension unless you control your obsession with time, money and refusal to adapt to change. Your aggressiveness needs to be checked before it burns you out. Life is not about aggression or swimming against the waves. Money and time are important factors, but they can't override human values and relationships.

20–25: Although you are not strictly in the Type A category, you teeter between the Type A and Type B. You strive for, sometimes ineffectively, a balanced approach, but you will do well to take it easy on some occasions. Life has so many beautiful moments and a person who is able to enjoy them has lived life the way it is to be lived.

10–15: Fantastic! You definitely don't have the privilege of belonging to the Type A club and thank your adjusting temperament for that. You hate confrontations and are mature enough to know when you should ignore things. Winning may be important but failures are the stepping-stones to learning.

The Final Word

Maybe you have learnt to get yourself more relaxed by the time you reach the end of the book, or maybe you haven't really mastered the art of relaxation because you didn't have the time to try out any of the methods given in it. It really doesn't matter. At the end of the day, it is important to know what your intentions are. If the intention is right, the work will be done at some point or the other. That is my belief! Just the awareness that you need to incorporate relaxation in your daily life is good enough for the time being. The rest will eventually follow.

We never find happiness by chasing it; instead we should simply open our hearts and let it pour in. How we choose to look at the world makes such a big difference. If we look at it through timid eyes, it's a frightening world. If we look at it darkly, we find nothing but gloom. If we look at it cynically, we're never at a loss for things to criticise. We can be against the world, or we can be for it. And when we're for it, it can be a wonderful place. Not every minute, of course, or even every day, but certainly most of the time. The ability of relaxing will eventually get you to your goal and smoothly, too.

Here are some beautiful lines that I came across recently. I would like to share them with you.

What Is Maturity?

- Maturity is the ability to control anger and settle differences without violence or destruction.
- Maturity is patience. It is the willingness to let go of immediate pleasure in favour of the long-term gain.
- Maturity is perseverance – the ability to sweat out a project or a situation in spite of heavy opposition and discouraging setbacks.
- Maturity is the capacity to face unpleasantness, frustration, discomfort and defeat without complaint or collapse.
- Maturity is the ability to make a decision and stand by it. The immature spend their lives exploring endless possibilities and doing nothing.

I would like to add just another line to these – maturity is the ability to withstand stress and know the art of relaxing.